Voyages

Denise McEvoy

Voyages of the *Dayspring*
Sailors for the Gospel

Ron and Aggie Russell
and
Denise McEvoy

Illustrations by Mike Dilly

Marshall Pickering

Marshall Morgan and Scott
Marshall Pickering
34–42 Cleveland Street, London, W1P 5FB, U.K.

First published in 1989 by Marshall Morgan and Scott Publications
Ltd. Part of the Marshall Pickering Holdings Group

British Library Cataloguing in Publication Data
McEvoy, Denise
    Voyages of the Dayspring.
1. Christian life – Biographies
I. Title
248.4′092′4

ISBN 0–551–01891–7

ISBN: 0 551 00000 0

Text Set in Baskerville by Prima Graphics, Camberley, Surrey
Printed in Great Britain by Courier International, Tiptree,
Colchester, Essex

Contents

Dedication

To my husband, Michael, for all his love and support. Thanks also to Ron and Aggie Russell, and staff at Bible Society, for offering detailed background information and practical advice. Without their help, this book could not have been written.

Certain names have been changed in order that the persons concerned remain anonymous. However, the facts concerning them are accurate.

Acknowledgments

Special thanks to:

Dr Raymond R. Rickards and Les Pobjie, for allowing me to use material from their earlier publications in this biography: R. R. Rickards, *Onward Christian Sailor*, The Bible Society in the South Pacific (Fiji, 1977); L. Pobjie, *Build Me A Boat*, Anzea Books/The Bible Society in Australia (Australia, 1977).

The Council for World Mission, London, for supplying information on the missionaries, William Carey and John Williams.

Allan Pfeiffer, Steve Burmester and Wendy Palmer, for sharing their experiences aboard the *Dayspring*.

Mike Dilly, Bible Society, for providing the excellent illustrations used throughout this book.

Unless otherwise stated, all Scripture quotations are taken from the *Good News Bible*, published by the Bible Societies and Collins, copyright American Bible Society, 1966, 1971, 1976 (used by permission).

Foreword

On a warm, sunny Australian morning in 1985 Dallas Smith, a member of the Christian Surfers' Association, picked up his surfboard and made his way down to the beach. He was enjoying a weekend's surfing with a friend, sharing his experiences of his recent stay aboard *Dayspring* – the yacht used in Ron and Aggie Russell's seafaring ministry in the South Pacific. Suddenly Dallas stopped in his tracks. A wreck had been washed up during the night and, as he got nearer, he couldn't believe his eyes. There, in black and white, he saw the name *Dayspring I*.

The small yacht was the first of three vessels used by the Russells. Although she had long since been retired from active duty, she held a special place in Ron Russell's heart – he built her with his own hands to take Bibles to the remote islands and isolated atolls which lie scattered across the vast Pacific ocean. Her maiden voyage in 1972 marked the beginning of a new era in Bible distribution. Since that time many volunteers, including Dallas, had accompanied the *Dayspring* yachts to coastal villages where people were hungry for God's Word.

A year after Dallas's discovery, Ron and Aggie Russell visited the United Kingdom as guests of Bible Society. Audiences were thrilled to hear the exciting tale of their life afloat, and their recollections form a major part of this biography. They are an extraordinary couple and their story is one of courage, perseverance and faith. Above all else, it is a testament to the love and power of the living God.

1. A Unique Ministry

It was a cold and windy day in 1974 and *Dayspring* was moored in the harbour of the old capital of Fiji, Levuka, on the island of Ovalau. Ron and his crew had taken their cargo of literature ashore in a dinghy, and were visiting the local markets while Aggie remained on board with her daughter, June-Ann.

Suddenly, Aggie heard a hurricane warning on the radio and she rushed to the deck to raise the alarm. But her cries could not reach the men who had gone beyond the harbour to the village hall, where they were setting up the equipment for a Bible meeting later in the evening. Aggie takes up the story: 'There is always a hurricane bay that people go in to shelter, but you've got to get in before the sun goes down, I didn't know how to get hold of Ron. I kept on trying to yell and each time the wind would take my voice away and, of course, he didn't hear me.'

When the men returned to the wharf it was well into the afternoon. Seeing Aggie windswept, drenched and in obvious distress, they quickly rowed back to *Dayspring*. On hearing the news Ron decided to head for the nearest 'hurricane hole' near a small local island, but when he arrived it was too dark and turbulent to tackle the narrow entrance. He thought it best to anchor for the night in deep water, under the shelter of land. The wind had already increased to 45 knots and the sea was becoming rougher, but if the north-easterly wind kept its direction *Dayspring* would be safe.

Then, in the early hours of the morning, disaster struck. The wind changed its direction to backing north-west and Hurricane Jan hit Port Vila at nearby Vanuatu (formerly the New Hebrides). The tail end caught up with the *Dayspring* crew and attacked them with all its might. As Ron battled to steer into the wind, the boat began to drag on the bottom. It was being pushed across the water, and Ron realised that his anchors had become entangled in their chains. Quickly, he sent his Fijian helpers to the bow to clear them while he remained at the wheel, his engine full on, ready to steer *Dayspring* away from the surrounding reefs. By this time, the hurricane had grown stronger and conditions were chaotic. The waves were tearing into the yacht and the noise of the wind drowned almost every sound, making communication between captain and crew impossible.

Aggie was in a state of total fear. She hated the sea and was clinging to the cabin supports, praying fervently while the men did battle with the elements. Being half-Fijian Aggie could speak the language of the crew and Ron suddenly realised that she could help by crawling along the boat to find out what the boys were doing and then relating things back to him. He begged her to come on deck so, despite her fears, she made her way out into the night.

'It was the most frightful time in my whole life,' she recalls. 'The sea covered me, it was just black, and I thought I was in another world. I locked June-Ann in the back cabin with a big padlock and came up wearing big scuba-diving goggles, because the rain was so severe that it almost poked your eyes out. It was so painful as the rain hit your face, and I had to go to the bow. The waves were coming over me and the boat was underneath – up she came, down she went. I had to wedge myself in between the cabin and the railings and then an almighty wave came over me and all I could see was blackness.

'The sea was covering me over and over again, and when I could, I yelled to the boys. They were all Fijian and it was good because I spoke the language – there was no way that they could speak to Ron from there, as the howling wind just took your breath away. It wasn't until the next morning that we got all the chains away from the anchors and we stayed where we were until the dawn broke. You can't sail in the pitch black and during those dark hours it was as if hell had been let loose.'

With the morning light, the hurricane eased and Ron was able to leave the wheel to check the damage. Seeing that *Dayspring* was in no immediate danger, he gratefully settled down to a cup of tea!

This close brush with death was one of many dangerous encounters on the high seas. Even in the most extreme conditions Aggie's faith has sustained her for, although she is no sailor, she is quick to point out: 'I believe, in these circumstances, that God is always near, because we are where He wanted us to be from the beginning.'

The hurricane season, from December to April each year, is always a force to be reckoned with. 'If the weather is kind,' Ron comments, 'the Pacific is the most wonderful place to be, you wouldn't give it up for the world. But a lot of people have romantic ideas. In fact, it is extremely hard work.'

Indeed, the area God has chosen Ron and Aggie to serve is not the paradise many believe it to be. Once the favourite haunt of such writers and artists as Robert Louis Stevenson, Somerset Maugham and Gauguin, glorious white beaches and turquoise lagoons abound and romance and history lie heavy in the air. However, the Pacific is the greatest ocean in the world, covering a third of the earth's surface, and its natural beauty hides many dangers.

The marine life is spectacular. Dolphins and flying fish are a familiar sight in the phosphorescent waters, but further out to sea the great white man-eating shark stalks its prey. The world-famous coral reefs are breathtaking but they too can be death traps, and sailors need all their navigational skills to manoeuvre a safe passage through them. Even on dry land the hazards continue for the deep water trenches of the Pacific, formed by the Continental Drift, give rise to earthquakes and volcanic activity.

The scattered islands and atolls that make up the sixteen small nations of the South Pacific fall into three main groups: Melanesia, Polynesia and Micronesia. The larger Melanesian islands, such as Fiji and New Caledonia, were once part of a continent which included Australia, and some have a variety of mineral resources. The Polynesian and Micronesian islands, including Tonga, Tahiti, the Cook Islands, and Kiribati (formerly the Gilbert Islands), are volcanic, coral or a combination of both. The mountainous volcanic islands, sustained by torrential rainfall, are fertile and yield starchy tubers, citrus fruits, or tropical produce such as coconut palms, sugar cane, rice and coffee. The low coral islands or atolls – water surrounded by narrow strips of land – are not so plentiful. The limited dry land areas around the central lagoons are only 200 to 400 yards wide, and nothing but coconut and pandanus palms can grow in the shallow soil.

Although the islands are becoming increasingly multi-cultural, three ethnic groups predominate; the dark-skinned Melanesians, inland dwellers of aborigine

4

descent; the light-skinned Polynesians, a sea-faring race thought to have travelled from Indonesia in ancient times; and the copper-skinned Micronesians, who have Asian blood. These people are predominantly Christian. Over 55 per cent of the one and a half million inhabitants are Protestant and over 21 per cent are Roman Catholic. However, many of the islanders live in isolated regions where access to the Scriptures is limited, so Ron and Aggie have to travel across vast stretches of ocean to reach them.

During the last seventeen years the couple have received a tremendous welcome from the islanders and, where there is a large rural population, *Dayspring*'s arrival is usually celebrated with ceremonies and feasts. 'They stir me, the welcomes', Ron comments, 'especially when the Scripture table comes out. When you have been in bad weather looking for a tiny little atoll you are very tired, but it all seems to be swept away when the villagers come out to greet you.'

The people of the Pacific were not always famous for their hospitality. Prior to the arrival of the Christian missionaries, the primitive islanders were notorious for their barbaric cruelty and ferocious hostility. The Melanesians followed the cult of the dead (ancestor worship) and some 'religious' practices included the launching of war canoes over the bodies of young living girls. The Polynesians believed in a variety of gods, including a god of war who demanded human sacrifices. Cannibalism, tribal warfare and disease were rife in many of the islands and strangers were usually killed. Indeed, long before Ron Russell sailed in Pacific waters many early sailors, including the famous English explorer Captain James Cook, came to a sticky end!

During the eighteenth century the intrepid Captain undertook three voyages to the Pacific, to gather information on the movement of the planets and to search for a fabled southern continent of great natural wealth. A man of many talents – physician, mathematician, astronomer and master navigator – Cook discovered New Caledonia and the Norfolk Islands on his travels. He proved once and for all that the mysterious continent was nothing more than a myth, but his explorations paved the way for some 200 years of British involvement in the South Seas. One of the outstanding names in western naval history, Cook suffered an untimely death at the hands of Hawaiian warriors after a short skirmish.

Not long after, another famous English seaman, Captain Bligh of HMS *Bounty*, also received a frosty reception from the islanders. Cast adrift in an open boat by Fletcher Christian and his fellow mutineers, the Captain and a few faithful men were chased by Fijian war canoes before eventually reaching the safety of Dutch Timor in Indonesia. However, that was in 1789; although many tribal customs persist to the present day, the savage pursuit of strangers is not among them.

This change is largely due to the dedication of men like William Carey and John Williams, two outstanding missionaries of the early nineteenth century. William Carey, a prominent Baptist who went to serve in India in 1793, was so inspired by Captain Cook's voyages that he wrote a book about the islanders of the South Seas, and encouraged missionaries to visit them at the earliest opportunity. There was certainly a growing need for some kind of Christian presence in the area at that time, for unscrupulous European traders and 'blackbirders', who kidnapped the islanders for slave labour overseas, were particularly active. Although John Williams, a nonconformist, never knew Carey, he evidently read the missionary's description of the Pacific. Inspired to offer his services there, he and his young wife set sail from England in 1816.

Williams was only twenty years of age but he was afire with a sense of mission, and eager to share his Christian faith with the people in this strange new territory. Under the auspices of the London Missionary Society he travelled extensively throughout Polynesia, from Tahiti and Raiatea in the Society Islands to Rarotonga in the Cook Islands, and on to Samoa. He once said, 'For my own part, I cannot content myself within the narrow limits of a single reef,'* and built his own ship, the *Messenger of Peace*, to travel further afield. Eventually sailing west to the Melanesian island group of Vanuatu, he was martyred at Erromango in 1839.

During his ministry Williams had a profound effect on the island people, teaching them to build homes, churches and schools, and helping them to draw up a Christian code of laws for civil administration. He also superintended the printing of the Rarotonga New Testatment, undertaken by the British and Foreign Bible Society in 1835. Williams was buried at Upolu in Western Samoa and his death was not in vain. The foundation stone of a monument to his memory was laid by a young Christian – the son of the very man who had killed him! Within a few short years the London Missionary Society, eager to continue Williams' work, raised enough money to send a new ship bearing his name back to the islands. Six more followed and the *John Williams VII*, launched in 1948, was sold to the Kiribati government in 1971 to serve the churches in that area.

*R. Lovett, *History of the London Missionary Society 1795-1895, Vol. I, p.256.*

The modern Pacific – the scene of bitter conflict during the Second World War – is a curious blend of the old and new. In the remote atolls, village communities run by local chiefs are still the norm and ancient traditions and crafts survive, but the larger islands are now firmly rooted in the twentieth century. Their traditional socio-economic structures, strongly influenced by European colonialism, have been further eroded by modern technology and international market forces.

The Bureau for Economic Development, established in 1973, has instigated a number of changes which have opened the South Seas to the outside world. The introduction of regional air and shipping lines has led to a growth in tourism and there has been increased affluence in some areas, but the winds of change have not always been kind. The growth in processing plants and nuclear traffic has given cause for environmental concern, and there is also a great deal of poverty in the Pacific.

In recent years much hardship has been caused by the dramatic fall in the price of the main coconut-based cash crop, copra. The islanders now receive little for this commodity and other tropical produce, yet they are forced to pay high prices for imported food and other consumer goods from richer nations. Because of this, the men and women are being driven to cities in the larger islands, or to other countries, to earn money for their families. The needs are great, as Ron explains: 'The villagers are a lot poorer than they were. Their wages have been halved in ten years. They often can't afford the Scriptures I sell, despite the Bible Society subsidy.' He and Aggie sometimes pay for the Scriptures out of their own pockets because God's Word is always welcomed.

Climatic conditions have also taken their toll, and the Russells have often been shocked at the havoc caused by the severe Pacific weather. Cyclones have destroyed crops and made thousands homeless, but the faith of the islanders remains undaunted.

Ron once visited an area devastated by a hurricane, and was deeply moved at the importance placed on the Scriptures by a people who had lost everything. He and Aggie work closely with the Bible Society in the South Pacific and during times of national emergency the Society is particularly active. In 1985 the Fiji Islands were hit by a series of cyclones which severely damaged the nation's sugarcane crop. Two Bible distribution programmes were launched and the response from the people was tremendous. One seventy-year-old man swam across a river to obtain his copy and another, from the Naviti Islands, hired a boat to get to a distribution centre after hearing about the project on the radio. More recently, Bibles were airlifted into cyclone-devastated Vanuatu following an urgent plea from a Presbyterian church leader there.

There are other problems, especially in the more densely populated islands, where the people are finding it hard to adjust to the norms of an increasingly urban lifestyle. In some areas there has been a rise in drunkenness and permissiveness, because the islanders have rejected their traditional values in favour of western materialism. Consequently, one of the greatest dilemmas facing Pacific countries today is how to develop a new cultural identity, one which contains the best of the old and new. Some have taken the route of political independence. During the last two decades Fiji, the Solomons, Kiribati and Tuvalu are just a few of the nations who have broken their colonial ties with Europe. However, many islanders are also looking to their Christian faith for answers to the complex problems of the modern age.

Young people, who make up over 60 per cent of the Pacific's population, are a particular cause for concern. Many face economic hardship in their adult lives because employment opportunities are not keeping pace with the rise in literacy and education. In urban areas the government is often the main employer, but there are not enough jobs to go round. In Fiji alone some 7,000 young people flock onto the labour market each year and, in the face of fierce competition, they often lose hope for the future, However, the Bible Society in the South Pacific has been particularly active in reaching out to this age group. As part of a world-wide Youth Programme of Advance, thousands of Scripture selections have been distributed throughout the islands in recent years. In addition, colourful modern translations of the New Testament, at greatly reduced prices, were offered to Fijian and Tuvaluan young people during 1989.

Ron and Aggie have a daughter of their own and they are well aware of the problems facing today's youth. In some respects, life is harder than it was in the 1960s when they were seeking their way, but Ron and Aggie have also had their share of doubt and uncertainty. Ron was once a confirmed atheist, unable to settle down after leaving the army, and Aggie drank to escape life's problems. Now, however, their ministry is based on the firm belief that God's Word can guide young and old alike and Aggie comments: 'No other book can speak to me as the Bible can and tell me the truth about myself. Many people have an emptiness in their lives which they try to fill in different ways, but the Bible can speak to them and point them to Christ, who alone can fill that emptiness.' Such faith is well founded. During a visit to Australia Ron's own niece,

Wendy, was given a new sense of direction while reading the Bible.

The Russells return to Auckland, New Zealand, during the hurricane season each year. Their home base is fourteen miles from the centre of the bustling city, and during her 'rest period' *Dayspring* nestles quietly in the Tamaki Estuary. The yacht's permanent mooring – a gift from Paul Anslow (pastor of Ron and Aggie's home church) and his wife Christine – is in Dayspring Way! This aptly-named road is a fitting local tribute to Ron and Aggie's ministry.

When the seafaring days are finally over, Ron hopes to run a sailing centre where he can share his love of God and the sea with the younger generation. Some may be eager to know exactly how a man who hated religion, and a woman who had lost her way, came to embark on a rigorous ministry in the South Pacific. For these young people, and for others as they chart a safe passage through the storms of life, the *Dayspring* story will be a source of inspiration.

2. The Early Years

Times were hard in the London of the mid-1930s. It was the era of the Great Depression and mass unemployment. Jim Russell had a wife and a young family to support and, to add to his problems, his son Ron was recovering from two serious childhood illnesses, diphtheria and rickets. Forced to move to the only accommodation available, a single cramped room, they faced a bleak future until help arrived from an unexpected quarter. Because of Ron's bad health, the Russells were offered a council house in the West London suburb of Ealing and they moved there in 1938. The move came at just the right time. Britain was on the brink of war with Germany and the centre of London, soon to be heavily bombed by the Luftwaffe, was no place for children.

Jim Russell eventually found a job at the Handley Page aircraft factory and during the next four years, his son's health improved. Ron and the other children, three older girls and a younger girl and boy, settled down to life in suburbia. Ron's parents were not religious, so he had his first taste of Christianity in the classroom. He remembers: 'Scripture was taught in our local school, and the Headmaster used to lead morning devotions at assembly every day. I remember singing the hymn "For Those in Peril on the Sea" and I also went to Sunday School occasionally, just for a lark, but I didn't really think that religion had anything to do with everyday living.'

Even Ron's formal education was short-lived. Like many other children living near the cities, he was evacuated to a 'safe area' and found himself living on a farm in Wales. He loved the great outdoors and, unbeknown to his parents, spent his time working in the fields instead of attending the local school. When he returned to London the war was nearly over and he managed to get a job at his father's factory.

By this time Ron was growing up and, like all teenagers he began to think seriously about the meaning of life. 'I spent many sleepless nights wrestling with the arguments for and against God's existence and then, one day, I thought I had found the answer. I read a news item about a bus which had gone over a cliff killing or seriously injuring the children on board, and I thought, "Surely the God of Love they talk about is nonsense! If there really is a God, he would never have allowed such a thing to happen!" I became aggressively anti-religious after that.' Ron also became increasingly bored with post-war Ealing and he began to look for an escape route: 'I decided that I wanted adventure and I remember seeing adverts in the papers, you know, "Join the army at 18 and see the world."'

The army seemed to be the answer for Ron's restless spirit so he joined the 17th/18th Royal Hussars, Queen Mary's Own, for a five-year stint. As expected, he soon found himself travelling to faraway places like Egypt, Hong Kong, Germany, and Malaya, but the day-to-day reality was less than glamorous. 'Army life taught me to drink, smoke, and the rest of it, but I had only been in for six months when I realised I'd made a big mistake. The main thing missing was the kind of freedom I wanted, but it was too late. I knew I was stuck with it for five years.'

Ron did have one brush with adventure in Singapore. During the bitter struggles for independence in the 1950s the British army was sent to quell the riots there and Ron found himself chasing a rioter through the streets. When he finally caught up with him he had a nasty shock – the rioter was holding a fire bomb in his right hand and he was ready to throw it! 'I could see the bomb shining in the sun and I didn't know what to do next,' Ron remembers. 'I heard a scream and a crash of broken glass somewhere in the distance, but neither of us took any notice – it was hot and I could feel the sun prickling my skin. It seemed as if we stood facing each other for an eternity, although it was really only seconds.'

Suddenly, Ron found himself gripping the barrel of his rifle and swinging it at his opponent. It caught the rioter on the back of the neck and he staggered before running off into the crowd. Ron slumped back against the wall, amazed at his reaction to sudden danger. 'I'd always thought of myself as a quiet sort of person, but I wasn't so sure anymore.'

When the riots were over Ron was returned to Malaya, where he continued escort duty to the British High Commissioner, General Sir Gerald Templar. The previous Commissioner had been killed in an ambush by communist guerrillas and Ron found himself in the front line, in the lead scout car which always travelled ahead of the VIP. The escort also included a large armoured car with a two-pounder gun, and a troop carrier with two dozen troops at the rear. But despite the obvious risk, there was no attempt on the High Commissioner's life during Ron's time in Malaya. Instead of danger, Ron felt only a sense of frustration and the inevitable boredom. 'There I was in the jungle in a little tent and the only things to read were a lot of sailing magazines. As I looked at them, I began to think that this was where the true adventure lay, in sailing. I was so keen that I began to save £1 out of my £3.10 (shillings) salary so that I could learn to sail as soon as I got out of the army.'

Some of the magazines told the story of Peter Pye, who had sailed the world in an old converted fishing smack called *Moonraker*. Ron was fascinated and so was his army buddy, Rex Mitchell, a regimental gun fitter who had once been a Sea Cadet. Together they decided they would buy a boat as soon as their army days were over. First they needed information so, whilst on leave in Singapore, they went to Raffles Library to borrow some sailing books. However, no sooner had they entered the building when a sober-faced librarian told them: 'Members of the armed forces are not permitted to borrow books.' Ron thought it was a crime, for the shelves were full of volumes on general cruising and coastal navigation, and he whispered to Rex: 'We've got to have them.' The two soldiers waited until the librarian was engrossed in his index cards and then leapt into action. A few minutes later they swiftly left the building with a number of the precious journals tucked away in their uniforms!

During the months that followed, the would-be sailors studied the books intensely to learn all they could about their new hobby. Ron practised tying knots on the end of his camp bed, drew navigational charts on odd pieces of paper, and plotted imaginary voyages. Both he and Rex spent every free minute of their time reading and planning for their future at sea. Then they decided on some practical experience, and scrounged odd pieces of timber, lengths of rope, and nails and wire to build a make-shift raft. Although still very much an atheist, Ron had an almost prophetic conversation at this time. One of the men in his platoon gave him some timber and joked: 'Here you

are, Noah! I hope you finish before the flood comes.'
Unamused, Ron quickly retorted: 'Don't bring that
stupid story into it. Men don't build boats for gods
who don't exist, we're building this for ourselves.'
Little did he know that he was taking his first
tentative steps towards his future destiny!

When their vessel was ready, Ron and Rex put her
to the test in a disused tin mine which had filled with
water, using an old grey blanket for a sail. They were
surprised to find that she really was 'sea-worthy'. Just
like Huckleberry Finn and Tom Sawyer, those celebrated 'rafters' of fiction, the two men were filled with
a sense of adventure. The stagnant water of the old
mine was a far cry from the Mississippi or the sea, but
they could float on it and learn how to steer and
harness the wind. Ron recalls, 'Up and down the
length of the mine and round in circles our little craft,
as crude as it was, gave us a sense of the real thing. Our
dreams grew so large and sweet that we could almost
taste them and Kuala Lumpur seemed to be a thousand
miles away.'

Soon, however, Ron was forced to come back to
reality. He was discharged from the army and found
himself back in Ealing working as a gas-fitter. His
first few months at home were lonely – West London
was full of people but Ron had been away for five
years and he knew none of them. He remembers his
frustration: 'The one thing I looked forward to was
saving enough money to buy a boat. All I wanted to do
was sail, and three times a week I went to the library to
read about boats and sailing. Often I stood on the
banks of the Thames, watching those afloat enviously.'
Eventually, Rex joined Ron in civvy street and the
two men hired a small dinghy for weekend excursions,
but their first encounter with the Thames was a

disaster! They launched the craft in the upper reaches of the river at Bourne End, near Henley, but they did not have the sail set the right way round. The dinghy crashed into a bridge, much to the amusement of an old fisherman who called out, 'If you put your sail round the other way, the right way, maybe she'll go better. It's aback to the wind.' Sure enough, when Ron adjusted the sail, the boat ran smoothly.

Once they had mastered the basic techniques, the would-be sailors decided that they wanted a boat of their own. They were on the other side of the river at Burnham-on-Crouch when they saw a seventy-year-old smack called *Daisy* on sale for £400. She was 40 feet long, gaff-rigged with her mainsail and topsail attached to booms projecting from the mast, and she had no engine, but they fell in love with her instantly and bought her. As the river was usually congested with motor cruisers and yachts, the two men made a habit of rising early to take *Daisy* around the Thames Estuary.

One day, however, *Daisy* would not turn to put the wind behind her and she went sideways through a cluster of moored boats at six o'clock in the morning. Many boat-owners slept soundly on, unaware that a runaway craft was on the loose, but suddenly *Daisy* hit the forestay of a boat, spinning it around. There was no damage but the collision brought the owner, resplendent in pink pyjamas, rushing to deck shouting, 'Are you mad? Isn't the Thames safe any more?' Ron knew that nothing would stop *Daisy* except another boat or the anchor. He decided on the latter and finally brought her to a standstill. It was a nerve-racking incident but he and Rex persevered for another six months to gain as much practical experience as they could.

The following May the two men set sail for the Channel Islands, the base for their 'round-the-world' voyage. It was not an easy journey. They were fog-bound in the English Channel for a week and then a gale split *Daisy*'s stem, forcing them to pump continuously while water poured through the cracks. Once in Guernsey they made tomato boxes, and even delivered a large motor launch to the Mediterranean, to earn money for repairs. On the return voyage, there was another gale and *Daisy* ran before a strong tail wind. The sails had to be hauled in to be reefed and as the two sailors struggled with the elements the main sail split down the middle. Although they managed to pull it down, they suddenly discovered that the sail on the bowsprit had jammed and wouldn't come away.

'I'll have to crawl out and try to cut her down,' Ron called. Rex was horrified but there seemed to be no choice. Ron remembers, 'The bowsprit was see-sawing with the choppy sea and I inched along it, my arms and legs clasped tightly around the teetering spar. The wind tore at my clothes and the whipping spray stung my face, but I could see I was near the tip and I stretched with my right arm for the halyard holding the sail. Suddenly, *Daisy* dipped into a trough and the bowsprit went under, carrying me with it. When we came up I was still clinging on, but my bones were frozen and my mouth seemed full of salt.'

Ron managed to cut the sail down, but despite the repairs the boat continued to leak all the way back to England. The journey so unnerved Rex that he refused to sail again, and Ron was forced to sell *Daisy* for a mere £360.

The sad end to the *Daisy* affair was a blow to Ron but he refused to give up altogether, and in February 1959 he invested in a 21-foot sloop called *Gannet*. Smaller and easier to handle than *Daisy*, she had one mainsail and another sail forward of the mast, the simplest kind of rig available. She was ideal for a lone sailor who wanted to take short voyages round the English coast, and every Friday night, as soon as the tide was right, Ron was away for a weekend afloat. He began to enjoy the challenge of looking after himself and was always in control of *Gannet*, even in the roughest weather. 'I sailed *Gannet* throughout that bitterly cold Easter,' he recalls, 'into the summer and late autumn, exploring every creek, river and harbour from Yarmouth on the east coast to the Solent.'

Putting his memories of Rex Mitchell behind him, Ron eventually teamed up with a new friend, Eddie Coyle. Eddie had no experience of the sea but he was cheerful and enthusiastic and in the summer of 1960 he joined Ron on a three-month trip to Denmark. The voyage was a success, and once back on English soil Ron and his new partner discussed the future over a pint of bitter. 'I told Eddie what I had in mind, to take *Gannet* across the Bay of Biscay to northern Spain and Portugal, through the Straits of Gibraltar and into the Mediterranean. I wanted to leave her in the Balearic Islands, making that a stepping point for future voyages. I intended to join her each summer and use the whole of the Mediterranean as a cruising ground.' Needless to say, Eddie was delighted with the idea.

However, the journey across the 600 miles of the Bay of Biscay was dangerous, particularly for amateur sailors. The Bay covers a continental shelf whose sea bed drops suddenly from 60 to 1,000 fathoms, causing tremendous upheaval on the surface in bad weather. Many sailors prefer to keep away from the area whenever possible, but this was the quickest route to Spanish Finisterre and Ron was determined to make the crossing. There would be no landmarks to guide him, so he had to learn the art of celestial navigation and he set about this task with his usual dogged determination. He managed to buy a second-hand sextant and strung some old rope across his backyard in Ealing to act as a false horizon, Ron spent many a cold winter's day braving the elements and learning how to use the instrument – much to the amusement of his neighbours!

The hard work paid off and Ron was ready to sail by the following May. He and Eddie went down to collect the *Gannet* from Poole Harbour in Dorset, where some last-minute repairs were being carried out. They were eager to get away and stacked their six months' supply of food and other necessities in the limited space available. Then, at the eleventh hour, the two men had a confrontation with a Customs official. When the officer came aboard to check the storage he told them to build a special locker which could be sealed when they set sail. Ron knew this was impractical on such a small boat, but the officer was adamant and hammered home his point: 'No locker, no stores. You damn yachtsmen are all alike – do you think I believe that you are going to the Med in this?' Ron and Eddie had no choice but to work all night to comply with regulations, but they were in for a surprise when their pompous friend returned the next morning.

He sprang aboard, shaking their hands heartily, and said, 'Ready to go, boys? I've got to hand it to you fellows, you've got more guts than I have. Here's your whisky and cigarettes – don't worry about a locker, dump them anywhere.' With that, he shook their hands again, saying, 'More power to your elbows mates, a good trip to you,' and off he went.

Eddie gasped, 'Well, I'll be damned', while Ron stood silent for a while, getting over the shock and thinking of the locker they had spent half the night building. Then the two men burst out laughing simultaneously.

Still grinning, Ron said, 'Get the lines off, Ed, let's get her away . . . and more power to your elbows, mate!'

Once afloat, Ron plotted the *Gannet*'s position with his new sextant. Comparing his findings with the dead reckoning, calculated with a compass and chart, he could see they were way out and told Ed, 'According to me, we're sitting on top of the Alps! I'm sure this sextant is no good, we'll have to keep a strict eye on our dead reckoning from now on.'

The boat sailed on for another six days, braving a strong gale to reach a position where Spain should have been in sight. When Ron climbed the mast he could see nothing so he returned to deck and picked up the sextant, but again his findings were wrong, so in desperation, he decided to head east. As darkness fell, the Spanish port of Corrunna came into view and Ron realised that the sextant had been right all along. He had simply miscalculated the strength of the tides in the English Channel!

From Corrunna Ron and Eddie sailed on to the small fishing village of Camerinos, where they spent a week moored in the harbour. Ron remembers the place and the people with affection. 'The first morning we were wakened by dozens of small boys who came alongside in their quaint rowing boats and asked for cigarettes. One of them, Pepe, became our friend and guide during our stay – he was about nine years old, likeable and honest, with a disarming smile. His energy knew no bounds – he would wake us in the morning with hot, crusty bread, then set about scrubbing the decks. Not content with this, he insisted on taking our dirty washing to his mother, who would wash our shirts against the rocks in the harbour. His one fault was his endless desire for tobacco and I honestly feared for his health.'

Pepe couldn't believe that Ron and Eddie had travelled all the way from England in a boat with no engine, and when his father returned from a week's fishing in the Bay of Biscay, the young boy gave him a tour of the *Gannet*. Ron can still remember this colourful character, puffing furiously at his cigarette as he told his father the story in fast Spanish and dramatic gestures. He probably exaggerated wildly, as he held the fisherman spell-bound until the climax, when he dramatically lifted up the boards and exclaimed, 'No machina!'

From Camerinos Ron sailed on to Cadiz and it was here that he experienced his first taste of the notorious Lavanti gale. 'I never dreamt it could come up so suddenly. It came at us straight out of the east and within minutes we were reefed down hard, heeling right over, lee-rail awash. There were just four miles to shelter, four hard, cruel miles of sheer hell. The nearer we got to the harbour, the fiercer the Lavanti blew, heading us all the while.' A large entrance appeared between two moles but as Ron sailed between them he was horrified at what he saw. The whole basin was covered in white, breaking waves which were crashing over empty wharves and there was not a solitary vessel in sight.

'My nerves were almost at breaking point,' Ron recalls, 'and I screamed at Eddie above the wind, "What in hell's name is going on? Where do we go?" Suddenly I saw a fishing boat standing on what looked like a solid wall and then she vanished into thin air. I thought, "Where he can go, so can we," and I put the helm hard up and sped into the fishermen's harbour. It was overcrowded with a vast assortment of craft, including three destroyers of the Spanish Navy, sheltering from the storm.'

Ron later learned that the Lavanti reached a height of 55 knots that night. The *Gannet* took refuge in Cadiz for three days before heading south-east for Gibraltar, but she had to fight against the wind for another week until Ron found a haven at Cape Espucel. Again he and Eddie battled on, stopping at Tangier before reaching the breakwater of the outer harbour at Tarifa in the Gibraltar Strait. Then disaster almost overtook them. Eddie was sailing *Gannet* as a freak wind suddenly struck her and sent her onto the rocks. Ron thought that she was finished but suddenly a Good Samaritan, a rusty old Spanish fishing smack, came to the rescue. Ron remembers, 'The crew launched a large rowing boat and in no time four excited fishermen made the *Gannet* go like a skiff. We smartly handed our tow-lines to them, and we watched as the nylon rope stretched and strained until, with a final wrench, *Gannet* shuddered and we were afloat again.'

The gallant Spaniards towed the boat back to the quay, where later in the evening they entertained Ron and Eddie with Flamenco music and local folk songs. Daylight revealed no serious damage so the two men set sail for Gibraltar. From there they sailed on to the smallest of the Balearic Islands, Ibiza, which was to serve as the Mediterranean base for future adventures.

It was in Ibiza that Ron met another 'larger-than-life' character. 'I first saw him on the foredeck of a large three-masted schooner. This short, broad man with a large red beard was holding a lasso as he steered his yacht towards a vacant berth alongside *Gannet*. From what seemed an impossible distance, the rope suddenly left his hands to land perfectly over a bollard on the quay. "Born in the saddle I was," he told us.' The man, a seventy-year-old American, hailed from the mid-west and he had done just about everything, from roping his first deer at the age of seven, to driving cattle across the prairie and wildcatting for oil in Texas. During the last week of their voyage, Ron and Eddie spent many an evening enjoying the American's stories until time finally ran out. Ron found a Spaniard who was willing to care for the *Gannet* during the winter months, and he returned to England with Eddie, confident of many happy voyages to come.

It was not to be. No sooner had they returned home than Eddie met an old girlfriend and decided to get married. Once again, Ron was without a sailing partner and he knew that the Mediterranean climate and winds made solo yachting almost impossible. However, all was not lost. He was a lone sailor but he could still fulfil a lifelong ambition: he could sail around the world alone! He decided to take the Portuguese trades to Las Palmas and then go south towards the Equator. From there he would sail to Barbados in the West Indies, and across the Caribbean to Panama. By mid-January he would be able to tackle the 1,000 miles of light winds and doldrums to the Galapagos Islands, taking the south-east trades through the South Seas, and reaching New Zealand by way of Fiji. That was the plan – a lot of sailing for eighteen months on a budget of £5 a week!

The *Gannet* was only made for short coastal hauls, but Ron decided to buy some new rigging and two 'genoa' sails in readiness for an Atlantic crossing. He found work as a labourer and spent the winter saving for his return to Ibiza. When he finally arrived he was pleased to see that the *Gannet* was in good condition. He repainted her and sailed to Gibraltar for supplies before heading on to the Canary Islands. Sailing alone was hard work. Ron could not leave the helm for long and, at brief intervals, he had to rush down into the cabin for food and drink. He hardly slept for four days until he made an important discovery: the working staysail sheet could be rigged to control the tiller while he went below! At last he was free to sleep and move about at will.

When Ron finally arrived at Las Palmas he was pleased to see Tom Follit, a familiar 'yachtie' face from the previous summer. Tom introduced Ron to Frank and Joan Georgenson, a fascinating couple who owned a fine 40-foot cutter, the *Alano*. Frank, a retired American timber merchant, had been an alcoholic for thirty years until reading an article about the English sailor, Eric Hiscock. Frank was so impressed by the tales of Hiscock's round-the-world adventures that he left his native shores to start a 'new life' at sea. He had been cruising for three years when Ron met him. The two men struck up an immediate friendship, and Ron was particularly impressed by Joan, who disliked the sea but was so grateful for her husband's new lease of life that she was happy to join him. Joan's loyalty was prophetic but Ron had no way of knowing this at the time – Aggie and the *Dayspring* were things of the future.

Although the hurricane season in the West Indies was not quite over, Ron left for Barbados in early October, 1963. He picked up a good trade wind and, when it petered out, enjoyed a few weeks of calm before it returned. On a good day the *Gannet* travelled 100 miles, but on bad days she only managed twenty. Whilst afloat, Ron developed a routine. He rose early to enjoy a quiet moment watching the sea, then had a cooked breakfast before he took the morning longitudinal reading. This was followed by a quick clean-up and inspection for repairs, until it was time to take the noon latitude reading. Ron spent most afternoons

27

reading or chasing cockroaches with his flipflops – the insects flew aboard from other ships and he once counted seventy-four dead bodies on board! He usually slept on the floor between the bunks, the safest and most comfortable place in a constantly rolling boat. Although it was a lonely life, Ron had two pilot fish to keep him company, and they stayed with the *Gannet* until he reached his destination.

One morning Ron heard voices coming from the middle of nowhere and calling his name. For a moment he thought his lonely life had taken its toll on his senses. Rushing on deck, he was delighted to see Frank and Joan Georgenson. 'Do you need anything?' they called. Ron assured them that he was fine, but Frank laughingly replied: 'You do need something, Ron . . . you've got no trousers on.' Only then did the blushing Ron realise that, in his hurry to go on deck, he had forgotten to dress and was stark naked! He waved his friends on their way.

Five days later he sailed around Ragged Point and into Barbados Harbour. 'Just before sunrise I tacked against a light air off the land towards the yacht anchorage, where two solitary craft lay offshore. Suddenly, a flag appeared from one of them. It was the *Alano*. Frank, as ever an early riser, was signalling me a welcome. With a splash my anchor hit the bottom and, after forty-one days of braving the Atlantic, *Gannet* was still and silent once more.'

Having successfully crossed the Atlantic single-handed, Ron enjoyed a few days in Barbados before heading north-west through the West Indies. Whilst at St Lucia he met Lord Robert Somerset, brother of the Duke of Beaufort and owner of a beautiful yacht called the *Trenchmere*. A true democrat despite his privileged upbringing, the aristocrat invited Ron to do 'some real sailing' and suggested he join him on a trip to the

Sandblast Islands off Colombia. It was a once-in-a-lifetime opportunity but first Ron needed money to pay for repairs to *Gannet*. He eventually took a job aboard a charter vessel in the Virgin Islands, and on his return left his boat with a Canadian yachtsman before flying out to Granada to accept Bobby Somerset's invitation. The men sailed to the Azores and Spain but Ron was suddenly recalled to England. His father had been killed in a road accident and Ron knew that he should return home to see his widowed mother. Once in Ealing his sailing days seemed numbered, but then an old friend offered him a trip to the West Indies by way of Madeira, and Ron accepted.

He ended up aboard the *Kotchab*, a 40-foot vessel owned and skippered by Dr John Franklyn-Evans. The only other crew member was Dick Pohi, a young Maori from New Zealand, and the three men travelled to Madeira and Barbados in twenty-three days. Once at the destination, Ron flew back to join the *Gannet* and begin the next stage of his world voyage – across the Caribbean towards the Panama Canal. He hoped to reach the Canal before January to catch the trade winds and get through to the Galapagos Islands. He knew that if he missed the trades he ran the risk of being caught in the horse latitudes, a belt of calms between the winds which could drive the *Gannet* around in circles for weeks at a time.

It was Christmas Eve. The wind had increased to 40 knots and 30-foot waves engulfed the small boat. Ron decided to haul in the sails and turn the boat side-on to the waves, letting her ride in her own slick. He went below but there was no peace. All night long the *Gannet* rocked to and fro as the seas raged. The following morning was no better, so Ron tried to read until he became utterly depressed – he missed the glamour of the *Trenchmere* and he missed his family. Ron recalls, 'My mind went back to everyone at home because it was Christmas and I knew my family would be together. I couldn't stand the inactivity any longer, so I thought: "I'm going to sail, I don't care how strong the wind is" and I put my oilskin on with a towel around my neck. But I did a very stupid thing – I pulled back the hatch and left it open before jumping into the cockpit. Then I pushed the helm down and ran before those 30-foot waves – but I didn't run for very long because, suddenly, a great wave roared over the top of me and threw me against the cabin side. I was momentarily knocked out and when I came to my boat was sinking! For the first time in my life I was really scared, because I thought I was going to die.'

The water was pouring in through the open hatch and Ron began to shake with fear. Suddenly, he was able to think clearly and take command of the situation. The small sail, lashed by the wind, was threatening to pull the mast from the deck, so Ron rushed forward and hacked it down. He managed to bring the yacht around so that it lay side-on to the high waves and then he went below. He spent the next two hours pumping the water from the cabin. It was dark before he had finished and he was absolutely exhausted, but safe from disaster.

The Galapagos Islands, 3,000 miles west of the Marquesas, fascinated Ron. Their wealth of flora and fauna had been the inspiration for Darwin's Theory of Evolution, and Ron spent two months exploring and admiring the natural beauty of this Polynesian paradise. He eventually sailed on to the Marquesas, an area of rugged mountains, jungles, and valleys. Again the surroundings were impressive, but when Ron met up

30

with his old friends Dr Franklyn-Evans and Dick Pohi, he soon realised that all was not well. Dick had had a serious disagreement with the doctor, and begged Ron to take him home to New Zealand. Ron agreed, and the two set sail for the island kingdom of Tonga.

Whilst in the Tongan capital of Nuku'alofa, Ron met a sailor who had recently been wrecked on the Minerva reef. He warned Ron to steer well clear of this danger spot and described his lucky escape in vivid detail. 'You don't know what horror is until you feel your ship breaking up beneath you on a reef in the middle of the night. Our vessel broke into pieces and we were left standing on the reef, water frothing around our legs in the pitch black.' The sailor told Ron that he and his shipmates were forced to live on a stranded Japanese trawler for 102 days while they built a boat from the wreckage. Eventually, three men were able to sail to Fiji for help. 'I tell you it was a miracle we got out of it. We lost a couple of men, and it took all our faith in God to sustain us over the long months.' Despite his own recent brush with death, Ron was not impressed by the sailor's religious beliefs, but he did heed the warning about the treacherous reef en route to New Zealand.

When he finally arrived at Dick's home town of Whangarei, on the east coast of North Auckland, Ron stayed with his friend's grandmother and took a job as a fitter's mate. The life was comfortable and he soon fell into a trap, spending most evenings drinking in a nearby hotel before eating a hearty meal and slumping in front of the TV set. Ron remembers, 'One night I was staring blearily at the television and I thought: "This is no good, I'm a prisoner, caught in a vice. I sailed on *Gannet* to find freedom, not for this." I knew that I had to leave so I decided to return to sailing and travel on to Fiji.'

An Australian workmate named Carew wanted to go with him and, although Ron preferred to travel alone, he decided to take a chance on his new sailing partner. He set sail in the spring of 1965, but his initial misgivings about Carew were soon justified, for despite a calm sea and a light south-easterly breeze Carew went down with seasickness for the entire 1,200-mile voyage! Ron was left to his own devices but the time passed without incident and the *Gannet* arrived safely at Suva, capital of Fiji's largest island, Viti Levu.

Within minutes of setting foot on Fijian soil, Ron and Carew were invited to a 'yachtie' party. 'When we arrived in Suva', Ron remembers, 'we couldn't clear Customs so we dropped anchor next to another boat. There was a party going on and it was here that I met Aggie for the first time, although I didn't really get to know her then.'

Aggie takes up the story: 'It was just another day and we were having a party on one of the yachts at the Yacht Club. A lot of people came aboard and Ron was introduced to me. I said: "How do you do" and that was it! I didn't take much notice of him – we were all having a good time, everyone was singing, and he was just another person joining the party.'

However, that brief meeting marked a turning-point in both their lives. Ron had sailed around the world single-handed but his days as a lone sailor were numbered. Soon he and Aggie would be charting a very different course, with God as the pilot.

33

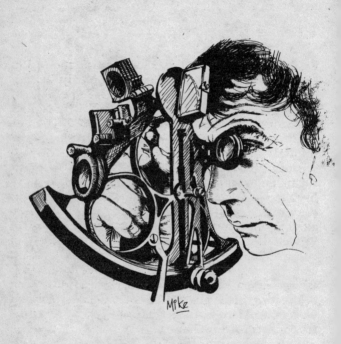

Mike

3. Conversion

Ron was impressed with the South Sea island of Viti Levu, home to more than 70 per cent of Fiji's varied population of over 715,000 people. It is full of natural beauty and has an immensely varied terrain. The south side, known as the coral coast, is famous for its giant sea turtles but, to the east, there are dense tropical rain forests. In the west there are green sugarcane fields and stately rows of coconut trees – the sugar and copra plantations which provide Fiji's livelihood. The capital, Suva, bears witness to the country's colonial past and the three-storey buildings along Main Street are reminders of a bygone age of British rule. The street markets reflect a variety of cultures, from ethnic Fijian to Indian and Chinese, and these add a splash of colour to the overall scene. Beyond Albert Park, where the Melanesians play their beloved rugby, the grand whitewashed mansion that is Government House stands high on a hill overlook-ing the coral reef of Suva Bay.

A few days after the party, Ron and Carew were leaving a department store in the city when the Australian suddenly pulled out a bright new under-water knife. Ron was impressed and commented, 'I didn't know you bought that.'

'I didn't,' Carew replied arrogantly, 'I just picked it up!'

Ron was horrified and retorted, 'Well, you just walk

back into the store and put it back! Yachties are welcomed in Suva, and the people are hospitable. We can't repay their trust by stealing.' Although he was not a religious man, Ron knew that the Fijians were a devout, predominantly Methodist people. He admired their shy, friendly manner and their respect for law and order. Carew, however, was unrepentant, and suddenly Ron realised just how much he disliked the workmate who had begged for a passage on *Gannet*.

Nevertheless the Australian was still with him when he set sail for Vanua Levu, Fiji's second largest island and home of the Great Sea Reef, the third largest barrier reef in the world. Once again Carew went down with seasickness and made a miraculous recovery as soon as the boat reached dry land. Emerging from the cabin he exclaimed, 'What a lovely place, when are we going ashore?'

Ron, who had finally lost patience with his sailing partner, replied, 'I've got news for you, mate. There's an airport here and you'll be on the next plane!'

Carew looked blankly at Ron and retorted, 'I can't. I've got no money for the airfare.'

Ron was dumbfounded. The Australian had promised to take enough money for a ticket home. Now Ron had no alternative but to pay the airfare himself and this left him with practically no savings. His encounter with Carew had turned out to be an expensive one!

With Carew gone, Ron decided to make the best of things so he began to explore the small planters' town of Savusavu. The town, which looks out on Somosomo Strait, is famous for its small boiling springs which bubble out among fragmented coral. The locals use the springs to cook their food. Within a few days, Ron had made friends with a number of local planters, accompanying them to the Planters' Club in the evening to drink, play snooker and discuss copra prices. One evening, Ron was called to the club phone and was puzzled to hear Aggie's voice on the other end of the line. 'What are you doing here?' he asked, to which Aggie replied: 'Why shouldn't I be here? I live here.'

Ron was surprised. 'What, in this little place?' The 'city girl' he had met on the yacht, and again in the streets of Suva, was actually a native of Vanua Levu, and lived with her parents just outside the town. Ron invited Aggie to visit him on board the *Gannet* and thought no more about it until the next day, when she arrived bearing gifts. Aggie had both hands full and explained, 'It's a steak and kidney pie and some buns. My mother baked them just for you as I told her you were living on tinned food.'

A few days later, Aggie invited Ron to her parents' home. Her father, Ng Wah Yee, was Chinese. He had arrived in Fiji as a young man and now ran the local village store. Her mother, Sera Levu, was Fijian, but she had a rich strain of European blood which could be traced back to the famous American, William Driver. Born in Salem, Massachusetts, in 1803, Driver was commonly remembered as 'Old Glory' because he was reputed to be the first to call the American flag by that name. Like Ron, he loved the sea and began a sailing career at the tender age of fourteen. He eventually became the captain of the brig *Charles Doggett* and sailed to the Fiji islands to collect turtle shell and the sea slug delicacy, 'beche de mer'. He was a pious man who refused to do any Sunday trading, but he succumbed to the weaknesses of the flesh and was known to have fathered a number of children by several Fijian wives. Sera Levu was one of his many descendants. 'Levu' was a nickname meaning 'big' in Fijian and Sera was large both in size and in reputation.

Years before, her great grandfather had taken the *Bounty* mutineers to a safe haven in Pitcairn, and now Sera was also famous for her Fijian hospitality. When she invited Ron to stay at the family home he gladly accepted, and he soon learned that she was a fearless, powerful personality who could sum up a situation almost immediately.

It was during this time that Ron and Aggie's relationship developed. Ron had sailed to Fiji for adventure, not romance, but as he got to know Aggie better, he began to feel a deep and genuine affection for her. Most afternoons they would go to the local hotel and spend their time drinking beer and talking on the verandah. The surroundings were green and lush and, apart from the occasional villager strolling by, they were left in almost total peace. Gradually Ron began to realise that, beneath Aggie's seeming zest for life, there lurked a sense of almost total desperation. She often cried and one day she told him the sad story of her early life.

Aggie had gone to the bright lights of Suva, where Ron first met her, to escape the misery of a broken marriage. She explained, 'It was a mistake, I shouldn't have married so young, not at seventeen. My mother told me it wouldn't work but I tried. But my husband was strict and he wouldn't let me go anywhere, not even to the pictures. He thought I should stay at home with my four children the whole time. The house was like a prison. I couldn't stand it, Ron, I had to get away, just for a while.'

Aggie told Ron how she had managed to save some money, leaving the children with her mother-in-law while she went to Noumea, in New Caledonia, for a holiday. 'When I came back my children were gone – they were living with my husband's family who would let me see them, but not take them.'

Ron found himself comforting the young woman as she continued, 'I turned to drink, Ron. I'd never touched it before but it drowned my sorrow for a while. I lived in Suva and kept ringing home, asking my mother for money, and every night I wept for my children. She knew how I was living in Suva and she begged me to return – she said I could do anything I liked in Savusavu, get drunk every night if I wanted to, as long as it was under her roof.'

The talking continued, and as the weeks passed Ron realised that he was falling in love with Aggie, so he decided to put his dreams of sailing behind him. The carefree life in Savusavu continued and one day the conversation turned to God. Ron remembers, 'There we were with a lot of time on our hands and I remember sitting outside and swatting mosquitoes, and we would talk about all sorts of things. We got round to speaking about God and I suddenly said, "Well, there isn't a God."'

Aggie, who had been brought up as a Methodist, thought that was absolutely stupid and said so. She described all the wonderful things even the islanders enjoy like the coconut, which produces everything for their daily needs. She told Ron, 'Look around you. All creation is beautiful, how can there not be a Creator? How can something like this world happen without somebody to make it happen?'

Ron was surprised by her strong beliefs. 'Always, even though we came home drunk once or twice, Aggie wouldn't even eat without saying Grace. Being a non-religious man, I found that absolutely amazing.'

Slowly, however, Ron began to have second thoughts on the subject. 'I began to think as a sailor. I knew that the moon controlled the tide and that if it were suddenly to shift, the whole world would be flooded. When I stood on deck with my sextant, I knew that I could use the stars and the moon to find my position all the time – a sailor could rely on these things to navigate a small boat across the world's oceans. I began to wonder if it really was just coincidence.'

By October 1965 Ron needed money, so he sailed to Brisbane, Australia, to sell the *Gannet* at a decent price. Throughout the voyage he constantly wrote to Aggie, telling her of his love and of his change of heart – he had finally come to the conclusion that there was a God after all. However, his new found belief wasn't a commitment and he had his own plans for the future. Ron intended to travel to America, on to Canada where one of his sisters had settled, and then to England to visit his mother.

Once on dry land, Ron couldn't sell the boat. Work was scarce, but he managed to find a job and continued to write to Aggie with his plans for the good life that awaited them. Then he met up with an old 'yachtie' friend who suggested that he advertise the *Gannet* in the 'For Sale' column of the local newspaper. The result was that the local journalists got wind of Ron's story and they had a field day! They turned it into the romantic saga of a man who had sailed the globe and couldn't return to his South Seas sweetheart because of a lack of funds. Such was the power of the press that, in no time at all, Ron had a buyer for his small boat and he returned to Viti Levu with £600 in his pocket.

However, once back on Fijian soil the money was soon spent on Aggie's divorce and other necessities, and Ron was forced to leave yet again, to take a job in a car assembly factory near Wellington, New Zealand. Aggie flew out to join him, working as a nurse's aide in Wellington Hospital until, five months later, her divorce came through. Sadly, however, when the couple returned to Fiji it was to a bitter blow. Aggie had not been granted custody of her three sons, and her young daughter had to remain with her paternal grandmother until the old lady died.

Things were soon to change for the better. Whilst working in Aggie's parents' shop, Ron met two Christians who were to have a profound impact on his life. The first, Maika Bovoro, was a Fijian Government District Officer who had seen army service in Malaya. He had become a sailor on discharge but, by the time Ron met him, had changed from a hard-drinking, brawling seaman into a gracious man who was an elder at the local Brethren Assembly Chapel. Maika was tall and dignified, but he also had a sense of peace about him and Ron was greatly impressed. He remembers, 'I always called him a walking Bible. He was a man that didn't say very much, but you wondered what he'd got that you hadn't, and I used to observe him secretly. A very fine man indeed.'

The other man was an English missionary named Geoff Harland. He always kept abreast of sailing news so that he would have something to discuss with the young Englishman. Occasionally, he would slip Ron a religious tract, but Ron wasn't impressed – he had already made his mind up about Jesus. He knew that Christ was a great spiritual teacher, but there hadn't been any Resurrection. Peter had been hungry for power and had made a religion out of the dead teacher, that was all. Then Geoff gave his sceptical friend a book on the lives and deaths of the early Christians and Ron was astonished. Peter, the tough man of the sea, had not only died for his faith, he had refused to be crucified in the same position as his master. Peter really did believe that Jesus was the Son of God. Had he seen the resurrected Christ as he had claimed?

Ron was finally convinced and told his friend, 'I

want to become a Christian, Geoff. I believe Jesus was divine and I want to follow Him.'

Geoff was cautious with his new convert. 'Ron, a Christian isn't simply one who follows Christ. You must ask the Lord Jesus to come and dwell within you. This is a personal thing. You must pray in faith and the living Christ, in the person of the Holy Spirit, will come into your life.'

At these words, Ron's enthusiasm waned. He had never prayed before and, like many other new Christians, he was too embarrassed to do so in front of his friend. Disappointed, Ron went home to Aggie but, as she was saying her prayers that night, he silently said the Lord's Prayer and invited Christ into his life. As he climbed into bed, he felt that something had happened. He remembers the moment vividly: 'Jesus must have come into my life because, the next day, I wanted to read the Bible. I couldn't put it down.'

Ron really believed the written words were speaking to him and he couldn't wait to share his discovery. He ran to Aggie and said, 'Aggie, I've invited Jesus Christ to come into my heart.'

Aggie, however, was not amused. 'That's ridiculous. How can Jesus come into a human heart? I've never heard of such a thing.' Aggie spent the next few days ridiculing him for his strange ideas.

One day, Ron had had enough and locked himself away for some peace and quiet. Aggie's temper got the better of her. Picking up an axe she ran screaming to the door yelling, 'You're not going to lock me out.' With that she began a vigorous assault on the wood, and Ron's sanctuary was suddenly shattered when the door burst open to reveal the axe-wielding Aggie in all her fury!

The arguing continued, as Aggie remembers. 'One night, Ron said to me: "Now, if the Lord Jesus wants me in the Sahara desert, I'm going to the Sahara desert" and I replied: "Well, how about me, where do I fit into your life?"'

Nevertheless, although Aggie was feeling increasingly apprehensive about Ron's change of heart and where it might all lead, she soon realised that he really was different. He seemed to have found a new sense of purpose. It had a profound effect on her and, three weeks later, she went to him and said: 'Well, I've done it, I've done what you've done – I've got Him now. I've asked Him to come in and change my life, and if He can change my life, He really must be the Son of God!' The couple began to pray and read the Scriptures together and on 21 January, 1967, ten days after Aggie's conversion, they were married at Geoff and Vivian Harland's house.

A week later, the whole village gathered to see the couple baptised in a local river, making their intention to lead a new life public and final. However, there were still many problems to be overcome. Aggie's friends made fun of her new faith, and because of the high cost of her divorce she and Ron were broke. Ron's special resident's permit was due to expire so he decided to head for New Zealand to find work, with Aggie following later. Although the couple did not realise it at the time, their life would never be the same again. A new chapter was about to begin.

Ron was eager to grow in his Christian life and when he arrived in Auckland he followed Geoff Harland's advice and moved into Eden Hall, a Brethren missionary home. It was here that he first met Jack Roberts, an army pensioner and an active member of the Seamen's Wayside Mission. Jack had been a 'bush-whacker' in the timber country of North Island for most of his life, and before his conversion, he had also been an alcoholic. The two men struck up an instant friendship and, during the weeks that followed, Ron often accompanied Jack on his witnessing in the dockland area. Occasionally, they came face to face with some violent opposition.

One night Ron and Jack boarded a ship and slid down a pole into the living quarters where some thirty seamen were relaxing. Astonished at the sudden arrival of their unexpected visitors, the sailors nevertheless listened to what the two men had to say until, out of nowhere, the cook appeared. He was drunk and began to hurl abuse, his eyes glaring and his fists shaking violently. Ron remembers, 'He swore at us and Roberts thrust a booklet and some Scriptures into his hand. We made a swift exit, his curses echoing in our ears, but when we returned a few days later the cook, now sober, sought us out and thanked us. He was a changed man. God had changed him – he said he had been a hard-living man but he had been converted after we had left him.'

On another occasion, a drunken seaman came at the two men with a bottle. Roberts stood firm, his face shining and, in a clear voice, the old man began to sing: 'I'd rather have Jesus than silver or gold . . .' The seaman stared helplessly at the glowing, singing pensioner He finally dropped his bottle and lurched away.

Ron enjoyed his outings with Jack Roberts but he soon realised that his own knowledge of the Bible was limited, so he decided to seek some Bible study. One Sunday evening he took the tram to the Town Hall to see Professor Blakelock, a Professor of Classics at the University of Auckland and a well-known theologian. However, Ron never reached his destination. While he was sitting reading his Bible he remembered something that the secretary of his church had said the week before. A Christian Literature Crusade lecture was being held at the Baptist Tabernacle that evening, and suddenly Ron had the strong conviction that he was meant to attend. He was a very young Christian and he didn't even know what a tabernacle was, so he asked the tram driver, who told him, 'Get off here and, if you go down Wellersley Street, you'll come to the tabernacle.'

Ron quickly left the tram and made his way to the venue. The talk was not particularly interesting until the speaker, a Welshman called Thomas, suddenly said, 'We desperately need somebody to get into Suva because we believe that the Lord wants us to open a Bible shop there – we really need a Fijian citizen.'

Ron, sure that this was his call from God, quickly made his way to Thomas and said, 'I'm your man – I'll open your shop for you. My wife is Fijian.'

Thomas looked at Ron and enquired if he was familiar with the Bible. Ron had to admit that, although he had begun to read the Scriptures in earnest, he still had a lot to learn. Thomas replied, 'It could be that the Lord wants you to do this, but you'll have to know a lot more about the Bible. Have you thought about going to a Bible school?' Ron explained that he was newly married and had been very busy, so Thomas told him to go home and pray about his future.

Feeling dejected, Ron went back to Eden Hall and took the speaker's advice. He need not have worried, for the answer came soon enough. The following weekend a Canadian friend invited him to go for a ride on his motorscooter. He took him to Capernwray Lodge, a Bible school in the quiet suburb of Howick, where Ron soon found himself telling the director, Tony Hanne, about his dreams of opening a bookshop in Suva. The school's three-month course was ideal for his needs and Hanne told him, 'There's a course starting in three weeks'. Everything seemed to be fitting into place, but Ron had not yet learned to live by faith, and he could only see obstacles.

He told the director, 'Oh well, Aggie is still in Fiji and we haven't got a home. I've got no money and I owe several hundred dollars to the Fiji bank. God can't pay my debts.'

Hanne smiled, and replied, 'If you want to come to our school, if you feel this is what God wants you to do, the Lord can provide your fees. The Lord is quite capable of paying a couple of hundred dollars.'

Ron was still doubtful but he was keen to enrol, so he wrote to Aggie to tell her of his plans. Both she and Geoff Harland wrote back telling him to slow down, but he was determined to go ahead. Sure enough, the money Ron so desperately needed arrived almost out of the blue – he received a large tax rebate from his job in Wellington, enough to pay off his debts and buy an air ticket for Aggie. He took his place on the three months' course and Aggie joined him soon after.

The world-famous Capernwray Movement owes its origins to a retired British army officer, Major W. Ian Thomas, who founded the first Capernwray Bible School just after the Second World War. Initially, the major and his wife purchased an old castle in Lancashire, England, to provide an international Christian holiday centre for young people. Later they introduced short intensive Bible study courses to help the young people read and understand the Scriptures. The aim was to encourage an understanding of how the Bible could reveal the 'living and indwelling Christ' so that students could become lay witnesses for their own denominations. The success of Capernwray Hall was such that similar centres were founded overseas.

The New Zealand branch was opened when the major discovered the ideal location for a new college – a large old house set in four acres of lawn in a quiet residential area of Auckland. He had been corresponding with Tony Hanne, a doctor who was already running his own local Bible study classes, and it was agreed that Tony and his wife would move in as administrators.

Ron and Aggie soon found that life at Capernwray Lodge was very challenging. There were five lectures a day during the week, and three on Saturday. Friday was work day, when students did odd jobs around the house and gardens. On one such day, Ron found himself talking to a fellow student while Aggie, always in high spirits, tackled her Friday task of window-cleaning. The girl asked Ron how he was finding the course. He had to admit that he found it difficult to listen and take notes at the same time. 'Aggie takes them for both of us. We go over them in our room at night – I'm not used to the lecture style of teaching and I can't always understand the biblical and theological language.'

The student looked at Ron, 'I hadn't thought of that before. I come from a Christian home and I guess a lot of the words and phrases have become clichés to me.'

'That's the point,' Ron replied. 'I like things said as they are, without the trimmings. Take yesterday, everybody arguing about baptism – whether immersion or sprinkling. The discussion was getting nowhere, a waste of time.'

The girl agreed and her words gave Ron a new-found sense of confidence in his own approach to the studies. She replied, 'Ron, you shut us all up when you cut in and demanded to know the motive, the reason, and the heart response. It made me see how much time we waste arguing about unimportant matters.'

47

Throughout the course, Ron and Aggie received a lot of encouragement from Tony and June Hanne. June, in particular, helped Ron to realise that he did not have to be a perfect model of a Christian. Since his conversion he had become very pious and intolerant of the shortcomings of others, but one day he heard a lecture on Colossians 2.6-7. The passage reads: 'Since you have accepted Jesus Christ as Lord, live in union with him. Keep your roots deep in him, build your lives on him, and become stronger in your faith, as you were taught. And be filled with thanksgiving.' Suddenly, Ron understood that God didn't want him to live by rigid rules and regulations, or be a carbon copy of someone else no matter how good a Christian they might be. God wanted Ron to be himself.

By the time the course ended in the early summer of 1967, Aggie was expecting their first baby. Tony Hanne allowed the Russells to stay in their lodgings and Ron wrote to the Fijian Government, asking for permission to enter the country and open a small Bible bookshop. Their reply brought disappointment for despite the fact that Ron was married to a Fijian citizen, the official letter stated that under no circumstances would he be allowed to reside and work in Fiji. Ron had no choice but to stay on at the school, working with a local plumbing firm during the day and attending lectures in the evening.

Nevertheless, the time wasn't wasted, for he soon received a unique opportunity to witness to his workmates. The Geering Controversy was raging. Professor Lloyd Geering, of the University of Otago in Dunedin, had recently published a bestseller entitled *God in the New World*. It examined the historical evidence for the empty tomb and the professor quoted one Scottish scholar as saying, 'The bones of Jesus lie somewhere in Palestine'. A court case involving the professor and the Presbyterian Church followed. Although charges of heresy were dropped, the controversy continued in homes, churches, bars and workplaces throughout New Zealand.

Ron's workmates joined in the argument and decided to challenge the 'pious' young man who always read his Bible at lunchtime. One asked: 'Well, what does the laddy in the corner have to say about it?' Ron prayed for the right words and suddenly he found himself talking freely to the men about the risen Christ. He had discovered a new talent that was to play an important part in his future Christian life.

As the weeks passed New Zealand was plunged into a recession and Ron was made redundant. The baby was almost due and things were looking bleak. Then Ron heard that a local factory needed an overseer and although the company had recently laid off half a dozen men Ron went along anyway. His perseverance paid off in an unexpected way. He managed to get a job next door, at a second-hand woodworking machinery business, but his spirits were very low. By this time it was obvious that Ron's dream of opening a Bible shop was not to be. Aggie returned to Fiji for a short holiday and he was left alone to contemplate an uncertain future.

Ron wondered how he could serve the Lord, and suddenly – the answer came to him. 'I realised that I could use the one talent I had, which was sailing. It was then that God said to me: "Build a boat." But I wasn't sure whether it was God or the devil, to be honest, because earlier in my Christian experience I had read a verse in the Bible which says, "Keep yourself from idols". I actually had an idol, and that was sailing. I had given that to God and here He was, it seemed, giving it back to me.'

Ron turned to the Bible for guidance and found himself reading the Book of Judges. He came to the sixth chapter, where Gideon asks, 'If you are pleased with me, give me some proof that you are really the Lord.' Ron decided to ask for a special sign from God – a sum of money to arrive on a certain date. He told no one about his plan, not even Aggie.

When the day finally arrived he could not contain his excitement, for he was sure that God would answer his prayers. But the money did not materialise. Ron had expected it to arrive from nowhere, and by nightfall he was utterly dejected. He went to bed but could not sleep. 'I thought, "I've fooled myself from beginning to end for the past six months. All the little things that have happened, even the peace that I have, it's all nonsense."'

However, with the dawn came a revelation. As Ron made his way to the breakfast room he noticed a brown envelope on the table in the hall. Instinctively, he knew it was for him. It was addressed simply to Mr Ron Russell, and his fingers trembled as he broke the seal. The postal note inside had been sent from New Zealand's South Island, it was for the exact amount he had asked for, and there was no accompanying letter! The cheque had arrived the day before but Ron hadn't seen it. Now he had the proof he needed to start his project.

After the initial euphoria, however, Ron came down to eart with a bump. He had never built a boat or anything else in his life, and he had no natural talent at carpentry to draw on, so he decided to put the money to one side and wait. The weeks passed and, after Aggie had returned to Auckland, the couple moved into a small house in Cockle Bay where their daughter June-Ann was born. By this time Aggie knew all about the boat but she was less than enthusiastic. She remembers, 'When Ron told me that he was going to build a boat I thought, "Gosh, this is going to take years to build, it's ridiculous, he's gone off his head!"' Aggie had been born in the South Sea Islands but she had no great love of the sea. She also had a young baby to care for and a boat was a far cry from the domestic haven she had in mind!

Jack Roberts arrived at the door one evening, and his first words were highly significant: 'Ron, the Lord has told me to build a boat.' Ron was shocked, but he said nothing about his own plans and asked Jack to tell him more. His old friend said that he had been praying for the Jews and believed that God wanted him to sail to Israel. He told Ron, 'I've come to you because you're the only Christian I know who has any experience of sailing, and I thought you'd help me.' With that, the old man produced $180, which he had saved from his pension to fund the scheme.

Ron did not know what to do next, and decided to invite Tony Hanne round to meet Jack. The three men decided to ask God for guidance on the matter. They each spent some time in private prayer until Jack suddenly got up, tears falling down his face, and walked over to where his overcoat lay flung across a chair. He took a bundle of 10-dollar notes from the pocket and handed them to Ron, saying, 'Here you are. The boat is for you. God wants you to have the boat.'

Tony agreed: 'That's what the Lord clearly told me, too.'

The next day Aggie found an envelope containing $160 stuffed into the letterbox. Someone had written, 'In the name of the Lord Jesus Christ, God bless you both.' She was beginning to realise that there was more to the boat project than she had thought. As for

Ron, he knew the time had come. Like the Old
Testament Noah, he would build a boat – a boat for
God.

4. Dayspring I

It was raining heavily and Ron looked gloomily at his three companions, huddled together under a tree. 'A great day for working in the open!' he muttered. Until the downpour, things had been going well. One of Ron's friend had offered his backyard as a building site for the boat, and the men had been up bright and early to start work. They were just about to dig holes for the shed footings when the heavens opened! Now all they could do was shelter from the storm and watch silently as the water collected in puddles around them.

Suddenly a stranger appeared from nowhere. 'Trifle damp!' he smiled. 'My name's Ewart Anderson, I hear you're going to build a boat, and that it's to be the Lord's boat.' Ron nodded and the man continued: 'You're going to need some transport.'

'I hadn't thought about transport,' Ron replied, 'but you're right, I will need something to carry materials.'

Anderson, who had a caravan business in Wellington, pointed across the yard towards the street. 'I've got a van for you. You can keep it. It's yours.' Ron perked up. The van was old, but it was in good condition and was ideal for his needs.

Anderson asked him how he was going to build the boat so he explained their plan. 'First thing, if the rain ever stops, is to put the shed together. Then we'll lay a cement slab floor, about 26 feet long. The boat's a ferro-cement one and it will have a tremendous weight when it's plastered. We'll need a strong floor to support it.' Ron knew exactly what he wanted and continued, 'I'll have a big, laminated wood beam set on the cement slab and the boat frames will be nailed to it. There will be battens nailed along the frames, from bow to stern.'

'How long will it take?' Anderson asked.

Ron thought for a moment and replied, 'Well, I hope to be sailing the Pacific in six months. We've only got a six months' permit from the council anyway,'

Later that evening, Ron spread the plans across the living-room table and went over them again. Aggie walked in and said, 'June-Ann's asleep. What are you doing now?'

Ron looked up. 'Just checking it all.'

She leaned across the table to study her new home. 'Tell me again, Ron, how big will she be? By the shed size, it doesn't seem as if she'll be much longer than a bed of lettuce and a row of carrots.'

Ron smiled. 'She'll be 39 feet long, 31 feet on the waterline. Her beam, the width, will be just over 11 feet, and her draught will be 5 feet.'

Aggie looked bewildered. 'It doesn't sound very big, but it will be a big lump of cement. I've never heard of concrete boats – doesn't concrete sink?'

'No, ferro-cement boats float very well,' Ron replied. 'It's not a lump of cement. It's a boat! Look, this method may be cheap, but it gives a strong boat which needs hardly any maintenance. It won't leak and it will take hard knocks. We have to put up a mesh of steel rods – a bird-cage – then the mesh is plastered inside and out.'

Aggie returned to the plans. Ever practical, she

asked, 'Where do we sleep?'

Ron pointed to the drawing. 'Probably there, in the stern cabin. There'll be a double bunk and a single one there. And here in the saloon, there'll be a bunk on either side. And right up here, in the fo'c'sle, there'll be two more berths.'

'But,' Aggie asked, 'what about a kitchen?'

'There's a galley,' said Ron.

Aggie looked at her husband in mock seriousness. 'Am I to be a galley slave, then?'

Ron laughed and continued, 'Here is the toilet and shower. The boat will be sloop rigged – a single mast with two sails, one aft and a smaller one forward of the mast. With modern aids like winches, it should be simple enough to control it by myself.'

Ron was blinding Aggie with science. Secretly she dreaded the thought of taking a young baby out on the ocean, and she remembers, 'I prayed silently in my heart, "Please Lord, let June-Ann be out of nappies before the boat is ready to go out."'

As the weeks passed, the boat's skeleton began to loom large in the shed. People came to watch and some offered practical help. Donations, however small, were plentiful and always welcomed. One day Aggie spoke at a women's meeting and she came home bubbling with enthusiasm. 'Ron, it was a wonderful gathering. People were so interested in what we're doing. And Ron, one dear, frail old lady came up to me afterwards and handed me a dollar. "Here you are, my dear," she said, "this is for one nail." For one nail, Ron! Aren't people wonderful!'

By this time, Ron was becoming increasingly enthusiastic because the Lord seemed to be providing so much, but then the gifts stopped coming and the helpers disappeared. Disillusioned, Ron told his church that nobody was interested any more and, in an attempt to rally round, they sent working parties to help. But most of the men had no boat building experience, so they did not achieve a great deal. Even Ron could spend only a limited number of hours on the project as he had a full-time job in the week. Gradually, the truth began to dawn on him – he and Aggie would be doing most of the work and it would take much longer than either of them had thought.

When the steel mesh arrived, Ron and Aggie went to inspect it and Aggie asked, 'What do we do with this, Ron, how do we make the bird-cage?'

Ron answered, 'It'll take a long time. We have to tie every intersection with this wire. It has to be twisted round the rods, cut and tucked inside. We mustn't let any wire end stick out.' Aggie thought it seemed simple enough. Ron continued: 'You can be on the inside and push the ties through to me. I'll twist 'em, cut 'em, and tuck the ends back inside.'

Aggie laughed: 'I'm the pusher and you're the twister then!' Ron bought Aggie some gloves and through two long winters they laboured on, tying the mesh onto the frame. The sub-zero winds swept through the open shed and their fingers stiffened with the cold. One night, Aggie stopped to rub some ointment onto her aching hands. 'Ron, I reckon there are thousands of these ties to be made.'

'Yes,' Ron replied, '9,000, I think.'

Aggie shook her head and sighed, 'I believe it!'

They worked on – push, grip, twist, cut, tuck... 100, 500, 1000, and always so very cold. Occasionally, they stood back to look along the mesh towards the stern of the boat's skeleton. There seemed little to show for all the hours and weeks of monotonous pain, but Ron's faith kept him going and he murmured quietly to himself: 'You know all about it, Lord, one day this boat will be in the water.'

Ron was waiting patiently at the end of the telephone trying to get through to his friend, Harold Moore, a civil engineer with a building firm in Auckland. He was ready to plaster the boat but he needed advice. When he finally got through, the voice on the other end of the line was not Harold's, but Morley Sutherland's. Ron could not believe his luck, for by accident the company operator had connected him to a man who was a world authority in the technique of ferro-cement boat construction. Ron explained his situation and Sutherland replied, 'I'm willing to help you all I can. When you're ready for the plaster, call me. Strictly speaking, our man's under contract and isn't allowed to do amateur boats, but your cause is different. I'll ask him to call and see you.'

When the plasterer arrived at the make-shift boatyard, however, all he could do was criticise, and he was never available when Ron needed him. Ron realised that he was not the man for the job after all, so he and Aggie prayed for help. They went through the phone book with no success, until Ron finally came across a man who was doing some building work at Auckland University. Len Hoyland had never plastered a boat before, but he was willing to try and he told Ron that he would not charge for the hire of the machinery, only for labour and materials. Ron could hardly wait to tell Aggie the news. 'It'll cost $220, Aggie, that's the exact amount we have in the bank. This is it!'

The job was a specialised one and Hoyland took great pride in his work. He managed to smooth out the irregularities in the construction and by the time he had finished the boat looked magnificent. Hoyland's part in Ron and Aggie's story changed his own future, for he went on to become one of New Zealand's leading boat plasterers.

The next stage of the project was the deck and cabin

and, once again, Ron prayed for the right man to do the job. He had no doubt that someone would arrive, yet the days passed and no one came. One night Ron received a clear message in his prayers: 'You've got two hands. I will give you the ability.' Ron looked at his hands – he was no carpenter, but he realised that God wanted him to do the work. He ordered the wood and began to draw templates (patterns of the parts) on paper before transferring them to plywood. Ron's job at the woodworking factory was invaluable, as he was able to use the machinery there for numerous tasks, and in no time at all, he had the beams laminated and installed on board. A local manufacturer donated glass for the portholes, and when Ron took an unpaid vacation to do some extra chores, money arrived anonymously to cover his lost wages.

Summer arrived and Christians and non-Christians alike came to inspect Ron's 'home-made' craft. Some were a nuisance, like the Bible students who wanted to discuss their new-found, half-thought-out theology, and one night Ron told Aggie, 'These constant interruptions are hard to take.' Ron knew his visitors meant well and he did not want to chase them away.

Slowly, as the seasons changed yet again, the boat's interior began to take shape. But it was long and lonely work, and on one cold Saturday morning Ron decided that it was all too much. He had a heavy cold and a friend who had promised to help had not arrived. Once before when Ron had been feeling low, Ewart Anderson had told him, 'You've got to stick to it. When I see the boat, I'm so encouraged and I know that other Christians are seeing it, but if you give up, then it's going to insult the Lord. If you really believe God's in it, stick to it. It doesn't matter how long it takes – ten, twenty years... a hundred years, you know, like Noah... as long as it's a witness.' At that time Ewart's words had kept him going, but now Ron was shivering and he had had enough.

He sat down in the empty hull and cried out loud, 'I can't go on. I just don't know how, Lord. Nobody's interested.' He climbed down the ladder and his foot was on the bottom rung when a hand suddenly touched his shoulder. The friend had finally arrived, but Ron growled, 'I didn't think you'd turn up today. Nobody's really interested – people are always saying they will come and help on some part, but they never do, they just don't come.'

The friend look at Ron sympathetically. 'We Christians have busy lives, Ron. You know that. Hardly a spare moment – Sunday is our busiest day. Saturday is the only time we have to do our chores. Come on, Ron, let's get back to the hull.'

As the two men climbed up the ladder, another helper arrived, then another. They kept coming, and by lunchtime there were twelve men helping Ron. They had all made their way independently and later that day he said a silent prayer: 'Thank you, Lord for encouragement. I know that you are in the building of this boat.'

Early in 1972, Ron left his day job to concentrate on the boat. By this time Aggie was working as a telephone operator and the couple always seemed to have just enough money for their needs. They took each step in faith, trusting in God to supply the necessary materials, and He never disappointed them. Once Ron needed a large piece of steel piping to support the mast. Later when he was out driving he noticed a pipe lying in the road. He stopped to investigate and realised that, apart from a little rust, it was exactly the length and diameter he needed!

By late spring the boat was almost ready, but it still

had no name. Ron prayed and tried to think of something appropriate until he came across a verse in the Authorised Version of the Bible, 2 Peter 1.19. It read, 'A light that shineth in a dark place until the day dawn and a day star arise in your hearts.' That was it, he thought, Day Star. Then he remembered that a racehorse had the same name, so he went through the Scriptures again, using cross references, until he came to Luke 1.78: '... the Dayspring from on high.' Dayspring – he liked it, but he was not sure that it was the right name.

The next Sunday he went to church with Aggie and the word appeared in two hymns. On the way home they called in to see Aggie's uncle and Ron asked him what he thought of the name. Uncle Norman rose from his chair and made his way to the bookshelf. He took down a book and flicked through the pages until he found what he was looking for. Walking across to Ron he pointed to a picture of a nineteenth-century sailing ship. 'Look, see that? That's the *Dayspring*. It was one of the London Missionary Society's first vessels in the South Pacific.' That was it – the final seal of divine approval. Ron knew that God wanted him to call his boat *Dayspring*, it was appropriate, as Ron comments: 'It's a very old fashioned word and I believe it means the very first light of day – of course, dawn is the revelation of the day, but this word is used in the Bible to describe the revelation of Jesus, the Dayspring from on high.'

Ron walked impatiently from the back lawn around the house to the street. He was worried.

'They're not coming – there's no sign of them. They should be here – look at the time, where are they?' He was waiting for the trailer to take the boat to the harbour. *Dayspring* had no engine, mast, sails or rigging, but she was finally ready to be launched.

Aggie tried to reassure him. 'They'll come, it's not too late yet.'

Ron wasn't convinced. 'But we'll miss the tide. I must get her in the water at midday – I told them that the time was important. And what about all the church folk who are coming to watch the launch?'

At that point the trailer came into view. The men knew they were late and rushed to load the boat. When she was tied up and ready to go, Ron took the lead in a small Austin car, complete with a 'boat behind' sign. He drove slowly, no more than six miles an hour, through the traffic towards Auckland Harbour but he was worried. Suppose, after all his efforts, the boat didn't float?

'I was keeping an eye on the boat in the rear-view mirror,' Ron recalls, 'when suddenly what I saw made me freeze with fear. The boat lurched and fell on her side. I gripped the steering wheel, waiting for her to crash into the road – she didn't, but I quickly drove onto the kerb and ran back. The trailer men were full of apologies, explaining that in their haste they hadn't locked the big rigging screws to hold the boat securely. I examined the hull and luckily, although a hunk had been chipped out of the concrete keel, the damage was only slight. I went back to the wheel but we had missed the tide and the boat had to sit on the ramp until midnight.'

It was an anti-climax. The people from the local churches went away disappointed, and only Aggie stayed behind. For Ron, it was a sad end to three and a half years of effort, for he had been looking forward to celebrating this special day. Now, it seemed, *Dayspring* would be launched anonymously in the dead of night.

The couple waited in silence. Midnight came. And then something happened. Ron and Aggie couldn't believe their eyes – they were surrounded by a bead of car headlights strung out around the launching ramp. Their Christian friends had returned and they were shining their lights in encouragement! The boat was finally launched to an accompaniment of car horns and cheering voices. Despite Ron's fears, she sat perfectly in the dark water. The celebrations over, she was towed to the local marina and Ron spent the night on board, too excited to return home.

Now that *Dayspring* was finally afloat, Ron wanted to take part in the annual Water Weeks extravaganza – a month of sailing, skiing and other water sports organised by the local Bible school. The boat had no engine, so he had to find the money for a mast and sails. In the nick of time, funds arrived from well-wishers and Ron was able to buy some Oregon timber. A friend, Trevor Simpson, built the mast – it was 42 feet long and very heavy. Ron was unable to fit it on his own so he asked a gang of local workmen to help, and they had the job done in no time. When they refused to take any payment, Ron wanted to give them something so one of the workmen suggested some bottles of beer. A Christian colleague was with Ron at the time and he was horrified. However, Ron had come a long way since his 'intolerant' days at Capernwray, and he told his companion, 'I won't give them the actual beer. I'll give them the money. It's their choice what they buy with it. What right have I to say whether they should have beer or not?'

Things were going well but *Dayspring* still needed sails, so Ron asked a local firm for a quotation. He was horrified when they told him that they wanted $600! Aggie said, 'We haven't got anywhere near that much!' but Ron tried to find a way round the problem.

They'll let us have them for $200, with the balance due in two months. We've got exactly $200 in the bank.'

Aggie, however, was dubious. 'But Ron, that's been specially saved for our needs when we're in the mission field, when we mightn't be getting a regular wage. It's not meant for now, we can't use it.'

Ron decided to pray. He was sure he should use his savings for this immediate need so he went ahead and signed the cheque. Later that same day, when Aggie was looking through the mail, she couldn't believe her eyes when she found that one of the envelopes contained a cheque for $200! The gifts kept coming, and by the end of the Water Weeks Ron had the outstanding sum of money he needed.

Dayspring performed well during her first month at sea, but Ron knew she would need more than sails if she was to survive in the Pacific. A friend had given him a Lister engine two years earlier, and although Ron thought it was too big for his needs he decided to ask his friend, Tom Mitchell, for advice. Tom, a Scottish engineer, often helped Ron on the boat, and he was enthusiastic. 'That's the engine for you. Once it gets going, it will never stop. It's a heavy duty engine – you're probably going to be moving from village to village and you'll plod along. You don't want something that's going to eat up your diesel fuel and it won't. I can guarantee it won't drink more than half a gallon an hour.' Tom offered to strip the engine down and take a look at it. It was in good condition and turned out to be the right engine for *Dayspring* after all.

Other Christian friends were equally helpful. Bernard Tolmi, a cabinet-maker, supplied the engine beds and a man called Dave Thompson, whom Ron knew from various prayer meetings, also offered unexpected assistance. He told Ron, 'I've worked for the government as an electrical surveyor and I feel the Lord has definitely called me to put all your wiring in. I'd like to do the whole thing for you.'

Ron was pleased but he had no funds and told Thompson, 'I've no money for materials. The Lord hasn't provided the means yet.'

Thompson smiled. 'Yes He has. I've just had a bonus of several hundred dollars. I think that will cover it. The Lord has told me to provide it.' Ron was overwhelmed. Thompson kept his word and finally, it seemed, *Dayspring* was ready.

All that remained was an inspection by government naval surveyors. They arrived ten days before Ron planned to sail, but no sooner were they on board when they began to find faults. One asked, 'How many flares have you got?' They weren't happy with the number Ron gave them. There were other things too. They wanted strengthening for the cabin sides, ventilated boxes for the gas bottles, casing for the electrical system – the list was endless. One of the men looked at Ron. 'Look, we're only doing this for your own good, you know.' They continued, 'That door isn't good enough, you'll have to build sliding boards to go in front of it. And the hatch, that needs a piece at the back to lock it. You don't want it to rip off in bad weather, do you?'

It was late afternoon when the two men finally left and Ron was heartbroken. He thought he had built *Dayspring* to safe standards, according to his own experience at sea, and he did not know about all these rigid rules. Now, with only ten days to go before his much publicised departure, he had to rip out all the plumbing and wiring. The cost of all the jobs would be at least $1,000, way out of his reach. Once again, Ron sat down and cried out, 'Oh Lord, it's Your boat. What are You going to do with it now? Is it really

Your boat, or is it all in my mind?' He had never felt so alone, but gradually, his thoughts were interrupted by the sound of voices.

He went on deck to find four men from his church. As soon as their eyes fell on Ron they knew something was wrong, very wrong. One asked, 'What's up? The boat looks good.'

Ron murmured. 'Looks, only looks.'

The man replied, 'Why, what's wrong with her?'

'This is what's wrong with her,' Ron answered, waving his notebook in the air.

The men studied the list. One whistled and said, 'But she looks so good, so sound.' Ron replied, 'Basically, she is sound, but she's not sound enough. There must be a hundred things wrong here, and it's going to cost a couple of thousand dollars to fix it all. Well, that's it!'

One of the men looked at Ron. 'No, mate, that's not it. Let's take it up with the Lord. It might be possible to fix it up.'

'But how long?' Ron protested. 'Not in ten days. All Auckland knows that I planned to sail in ten days. Now I've got to go back to building the boat again and it could take months!'

Ron was in despair but he knew there was nowhere to turn except to God, so the five men prayed. When they had finished Ron felt calmer. He knew everything would work out, but he did not realise how quickly!

Throughout the whole of the following week *Dayspring* was crammed with people. They were everywhere – hammering, sawing, singing, laughing, asking questions – all helping to put *Dayspring* right. Ron took the job of overseer, notebook in hand, making his way through the crowded boat to give advice on how different jobs should be done. He told his church about the probable cost of all the alterations and said, 'I don't have the money but I'll go ahead to the limit of our savings and buy what I can. When I haven't got any more money, we'll just have to wait. I won't leave until everything's paid for. I won't leave a debt behind me.' Ron needn't have worried - the money came in, except for the final $700.

Before the ten days were up, he asked the surveyors to return. They were astonished at the changes and asked, 'How did you do it? Just how did you do it in less than two weeks?'

Ron smiled. 'Well, the Lord's people here in Auckland just gathered around and it was done.'

The two surveyors shook their heads and departed, wondering at it all. More surprises followed. When Ron went to pay off all his bills at the local store they had no record of his debt. The account had been closed and Ron came away with $700 to spare!

By May 1972 *Dayspring* was ready to sail. First Ron had to find a crew. He had plenty of offers, but he settled for four Christians who had helped to build his boat. They were Ewart Anderson, Bernard Tolmi, Rodney McCracken, from Ron's church, and Lance Harding. Then Ron learned that Tom Mitchell wanted to join the team – Tom wasn't a Christian, but he had given valuable help over the years, so he became the fifth crew member. The six men sailed out of Auckland Harbour, en route for Fiji, on 19 May and Aggie and June-Ann waved goodbye from the wharf. They planned to fly out to join Ron at a later date.

Dayspring was on her way, but the weather was rough and the novice sailors were no match for the elements. For the first five days Ron had to steer alone while his shipmates vomited, groaned, and lay helpless below deck. They managed to pull themselves together for the remainder of the trip and reached Suva on the eleventh day. Tom Mitchell was profoundly moved by the whole experience and later visited the Pakuranga Gospel Chapel in Auckland to tell of his experiences. Standing in front of the congregation he said, 'I would never have believed that six men could be together under those conditions, could vomit over each other, and yet never utter a cross word. It's made an everlasting impression on me.' Three months later, Tom became a Christian.

The maiden voyage over, Ron found himself in Suva once again. He had actually been advised not to go there because Fiji had just gained independence from Britain, and many expatriots were being asked to leave. It seemed he had little chance of getting a work permit, but Ron was convinced that God wanted him in Suva so he waited for something to develop. Weeks passed, nothing happened, and Ron began to worry. Then one day he found himself sitting in Victoria Arcade drinking coffee. It was an open-air arcade, edged with small shops, and there were offices off the first floor balcony. Ron did not know what to do next so, as he had done often in the past, he dropped his head in his hands and prayed silently, 'Lord, what do I do now?'

Suddenly, he heard a voice. 'Hello, Ron Russell. What are you doing here?' Ron looked up. It was an old friend, Foster Crane, a Brethren missionary who had been in Fiji for more than twenty-five years. Crane often helped other missionaries obtain permits and he sat down and listened to Ron's story. After a while he said, 'There's no hope at this stage. There just isn't any hope of you getting a permit.'

Ron was disappointed. He changed the subject and started to talk about people he had known in Savusavu. He asked. 'Where's Maika these days?'

Crane pointed upwards. 'He's up there.'

Ron looked at the sky and asked, 'What do you mean, up there?'

However, Maika hadn't gone to meet his Maker! Crane pointed again, towards the offices on the balcony, and explained. 'Up there. Didn't you know? He's head of the Bible Society here.'

Ron was excited. 'That's wonderful. Is his office up there?'

Crane nodded. 'Yes, on the verandah – the office and bookshop of the Bible Society.' Ron said goodbye to Crane and rushed upstairs.

He walked into the cramped offices where Maika Bovoro sat with his small staff, a typist and a boy who handled the storage and despatch of Scriptures to the South Pacific. Ron stretched out his hand. 'Hello, Maika.'

His old friend looked up and broke into a smile: 'Ron Russell! Where have you come from?'

Ron explained about *Dayspring* and then listened carefully as Maika described the urgent need to reach remote islanders with the Word of God. Maika told him, 'I've been praying for a way to reach the islands.'

Ron was excited. 'You mean you've been praying for the means to distribute Scriptures to the people of the Pacific?'

Maika understood what Ron was getting at. 'Yes, and you've been praying to learn what the *Dayspring* is meant to do!'

Suddenly Ron realised that he could provide a Bible bookshop after all – not in Suva, but throughout the eight and a half million square miles of the Pacific served by the Bible Society. The two men realised that their meeting was no accident. An 'unseen hand' had brought them together at the exact moment when each needed the other. Immediately, Ron and Malka committed the project to God.

At this time the Society was not autonomous, but operated under the Bible Society in New Zealand. Maika had to refer to its Secretary, the Rev. David Cohen, for approval of the *Dayspring* venture. Needless to say Cohen, an Australian, was enthusiastic and he visited Suva soon after to discuss details. Ron told him, 'I must confess that I don't know much about the Bible Society. I can't pretend that I've been an active follower at all. It's been just another organisation to me.'

Cohen looked at Ron and replied, 'It's the Gospel of Jesus Christ that counts and if we can help you to get out there to reach the people, and if you can distribute Bibles at the same time, well, that's worthwhile.'

David Cohen, now Scripture Union's General Director for England and Wales, recalls, 'I can remember vividly the meeting we had with Maika Bovoro, when the possibility opened up for Ron and Aggie to join our team in distributing Scriptures throughout the South Pacific. There is very little I can say about the part I played in the story. I guess I was responsible for perceiving their potential, and matching that with the needs that confronted us in the South Pacific – for an effective distribution network there. Ron and Aggie are unique, individually and as a couple.'

Initially Ron didn't want any financial help from the Bible Society as he planned to live entirely by faith. However, because of work permit requirements, he agreed to accept a monthly amount for expenses. The money would cover diesel fuel for the engine and other running costs, and each year the sum would be adjusted in line with cost-of-living rises. Ron was also supported by his church, the Tamiki Assembly in Auckland, by its offshoot, the Pakuranga Assembly, and by the Bible school's missionary fellowship. With all the details worked out, Maika applied for a work permit for Ron, and set about contacting all the churches in Fiji to seek letters of recommendation. Church backing, together with a definite job, would help to persuade the authorities that Ron's mission was a worthy one.

While he was waiting for everything to be settled, Ron decided to take *Dayspring* on a familiarisation tour of the Fiji islands. He had a visitor's permit and, although he wasn't allowed to preach publicly, he was free to enjoy fellowship with the islanders. With Aggie, June-Ann and two Bible students, he set sail for the Yasawa Group in Fiji's Western Division. On the way Ron stopped at Lautoka on the north-western coast of Viti Levu and it was here that he had his first meeting with Craig Whitley. Craig, an American, was scrubbing his ferro-cement boat as *Dayspring* arrived, and the students decided to give him a hand. He was grateful and later that evening called over to his helpers, 'I'm going to find a couple of birds. Would you like to join me?' Politely, the students declined. They heard him return in the early hours of the morning, drunk and singing at the top of his voice. The next day, *Dayspring* sailed on to the Yasawas, but when the crew returned to Lautoka, Whitley was still there.

One night Ron and the students were about to start their Bible study when, once again, Whitley came on board. 'I'm just going into town for a drink. Would you boys like to join me?'

Ron was annoyed and said, 'We're doing our Bible study. Perhaps you'd like to join us!'

He was not prepared for what happened next. Whitley replied in his broad Southern accent, 'I'd love to. I'd be delighted.' With that, he sat down and entered fully into the spirit of the occasion.

70

As Ron went deeper into the text, the group began to discuss Christ's death on the cross. Ron remembers, 'Suddenly, Whitley's face changed. He began to pray, pouring his heart out to God. Later that night as Aggie and I rowed him back to his boat, he explained that he had been converted at an early age, but had drifted into bad company. He had even been in prison and told us, "I've been an absolute backslider until this evening on your boat. Would you help me rededicate my life, here, tonight?"

'We knelt in Whitley's cabin and, with tears flowing freely, he invited Christ back into his life. Some time later, he wrote and told us about his run-in with a hurricane. When the storm attacked his small boat he wasn't frightened at all – he had regained his sense of inner peace.'

Ron's work permit finally came through on the day before his visitor's permit was due to expire, but there was a snag: because he was a British citizen, he had to put up a bond equal to the fare to England. He just did not have the necessary $1,000 and did not know where to get it. In desperation he asked Aggie if one of her relatives would give him a loan. She replied, 'They would gladly lend it, but we're not going to ask them. The Lord has brought us this far and, if He wants us to do the work, He will surely provide all the means.'

Ron knew Aggie was right and he suddenly realised that there was a solution. 'Aggie, it's all right, we don't have to find the fare to England. I'm a New Zealander!'

Ron remembered that, six months earlier when Aggie had applied for New Zealand citizenship, the authorities had offered him the same nationality as his wife. He actually possessed a certificate which proved he was a citizen, so he quickly took it to the Fijian authorities. On his arrival at the offices, however, Ron found that he still had one final hurdle to overcome. The official behind the counter told him, 'That's not good enough. You have to own a New Zealand passport.' Determined not to be beaten, Ron made his way to the New Zealand High Commissioner's office and explained his predicament. The next morning, he returned to the official with his newly-issued passport. At last Ron was ready to sail the Pacific.

He and Aggie were to be a formidable team in the Lord's service. At sea, he would use his seamanship to guide his boat safely to its destination. On land, she would use her knowledge of the islanders and their customs to prevent any misunderstandings. In their home-made boat, the couple would spend the next five years visiting islands large and small, each with its own languages and traditions, to spread the Good News of Jesus Christ. The *Dayspring* ministry had finally begun!

5. The Living Word

Ron turned on the radio. Hurricane Bebe was south of Rotuma, just 199 miles away, and it was heading straight for *Dayspring!* He went back on deck and struggled at the helm as the boat pitched into the heavy seas. The wind was whistling through the rigging. 'It's lucky Aggie isn't here,' he thought. They had been to Savusavu to visit her parents and Aggie and June-Ann had flown on to Suva to get things ready for their first Bible Society voyage. Ron and his crew, two Bible students, were just over 100 miles from the safety of Suva harbour but time was running out.

As *Dayspring* smashed into the waves the students were overcome by seasickness. They were terrified and wanted to disappear into the safety of the cabin, but Ron needed their help. He called out, 'Can you get out there and tie everything down securely? Make it tight, we're in for a rough time.' The boys pulled themselves together and managed to tie down the buckets, oars and anchor – anything that could be blown loose. The wind howled all around them as they crawled slowly back to the cockpit and fell exhausted onto the floor. Ron remained at the wheel, his eyes straining into the blackness of the night, as he tried to keep *Dayspring* on course.

Suddenly a grating, thudding noise startled him. A dark object sped across the deck before disappearing into the sea. Ron leaned forward and something else moved in the darkness. Loud bangs followed, and a long, thin object scraped across the boards. Ron realised what was happening and cried out, 'The oars!' The dinghy's oars had blown loose, but they were not the only things that were moving, for the wind and water were sweeping everything clear. There was nothing Ron could do except wait for daylight. When it came, he realised he had lost everything except the anchor.

By now, the wind had increased to 40 knots and, suddenly even the anchor went whipping through the air. It crashed into the green railing, breaking the iron stanchion and taking some cement with it. The blow left a crack in *Dayspring*'s hull and water began to pour in. Ron woke the students from their sleep, shouting anxiously, 'Check the bilges, pump her out.' Weakly the two boys groped for support and made their way to the pump, but as they worked it, nothing happened. It seemed that no water had got into the bilges after all.

Ron was almost at Suva now, just outside a narrow passage into the harbour. The opening was a tricky one and the waves were breaking dangerously through it, but there was nowhere else to go. According to the radio Bebe had swept through Funafuti in Tuvalu (formerly the Ellice Islands) with a velocity of 140 knots and Ron knew that *Dayspring* could never weather such a storm. Starting the Lister engine, he asked the students to pull the mainsail down and put up the smallest headsail on board. It was a struggle but they finally managed to get it up as *Dayspring* entered quieter waters.

But Ron's troubles weren't over. He looked into the cabin and found everything awash with oil and water. He screamed, 'For goodness sake, find out what the trouble is.' One of the boys suddenly noticed that the bilge was full of water and sodden cardboard. Ron cried out in desperation, 'The boxes, they've become papier-mache! Soggy cardboard has been sucked into the pump – that's why no water came out when you pumped. It's blocked!' On closer inspection, Ron could see that the papier-mache had also penetrated the engine, blocking all the filters. The resulting oil pressure had burst the pipes and this had caused the flooding in the cabin.

The boat was in a sorry state but at least Ron had reached the harbour. It was crowded with vessels of all types as he made his way towards a safe berth. When Bebe finally caught up with him, she had calmed to 100 knots but she was still a powerful force to be reckoned with. At one stage a yacht, blown to and fro by the wind, swayed perilously close to *Dayspring*. One of the students rushed to the railing, shouting, 'Hey, she's going to hit us this time!' He stretched out his arms as if to fend off the swinging boat, but Ron could see the danger and lunged forward to pull the student away a split second before the renegade craft smashed into *Dayspring*'s bow. 'You nearly had your arm crushed,' he exclaimed. The student went a deathly white as Ron inspected the damage. The bow was mangled and the railing had been twisted and partly torn out by the sheer force of the collision.

The strong winds, accompanied by torrential rain, continued for several days. In Fiji alone, Bebe killed nineteen people, injured hundreds, and left some 50,000 homeless. Entire villages were destroyed. Ron and Aggie weathered the storm but it left them with a heavy debt – the engine repairs totalled $200 and they were down to their last $20. Ron was about to set off on a six weeks' tour of Viti Levu and he was anxious not to leave any unpaid bills behind. He seemed to have no choice but then, at the eleventh hour, unexpected help arrived. On the very day Ron planned to sail, and just as he was preparing to pull up anchor, a man called to him from the shore, 'I've got some money for you.' The visitor had an anonymous cheque – for exactly $200!

Dayspring's first official tour was along the Rewa River to Gau Island and the islands of Bau, home of the paramount chiefs of Fiji. The people of Gau had asked Maika to prepare some Bible studies for them and, because communications had been severely damaged by Hurricane Bebe, Maika asked Ron to make an emergency trip.

Aggie was eager to begin her new life afloat. She recalls, 'I suppose, as they say, ignorance is bliss. Because I was so ignorant of the sea and how to live on a boat, it didn't worry me. I just went to it blindly and it was wonderful because I felt it was obedience to God.' However, Aggie was in for a rude awakening. After only a few days at sea she had her first attack of seasickness. It was a cross she would have to bear for many years to come but, despite her discomfort, the voyage proved to be a significant breakthrough for the Bible Society. Ron and Maika visited the Talatala, one of the two chiefs of Gau, and presented him with a tabua, a highly polished sperm whale's tooth. This symbol of plenty is usually presented to honoured guests of high rank, and the chief's acceptance of it gave the Bible Society freedom to visit all the villages under his control.

Wherever they went, Ron, Maika and Aggie were given the traditional Fijian welcome which included the Kava ceremony – the ritual preparation of a drink made from the green root of the pepper plant – and dancing and feasting. For an Englishman from west London, the hospitality of the South Sea islanders was an eye-opener and Ron has fond memories of these early days: 'When we first visited the islands we landed where and when we wanted, and spent hours being welcomed by the village leader. We were always allowed to set up shop in the local hall to show gospel films, give testimonies, and sell Bibles and Scripture items.'

The chief, the local minister and other important men of the village would make speeches, and to each of them Ron had to give a reply. When Maika was not with him Ron found Aggie's help invaluable. She was no sailor but, on dry land her islander blood and jovial personality made her the perfect 'ice-breaker'. She knew how to communicate effectively with the people and this special gift would become an important part of the *Dayspring* ministry. She explains, 'I am the talking chief – in island culture there is the real chief, who makes all the decisions, and the talking chief, who implements them. Ron gets us to our destination but then I look after the protocol and behaviour on shore, because different islands have different cultures and customs.'

Initially, Ron found it hard to adjust to the easy-going lifestyle, where meetings started much later than planned and discussions went on into the early hours. But, even after a late night, he and Aggie would be up bright and early to sail to the next village and set up their Bible and book display. The children would crowd around, eager to get Scripture portions or gospels for a few cents begged from their parents. 'The Fijians are a God-fearing people,' Aggie points out. 'They want to come around the Bible table and have God's Word reach their shores – they feel very honoured.' Often a meeting would be arranged for that evening. Films were a great attraction and the whole village would cram into the church or school hall.

Although the couple were working closely with the Bible Society in the South Pacific, they quickly developed their own personal ministry, sharing their faith and answering questions about the Bible. Aggie began to realise that many of the women needed help. 'Some were really lost and didn't know what it meant to be a committed Christian, to have a personal relationship with Jesus Christ. Sometimes there were marriage problems – the husbands went out and drank Kava all night and got intoxicated enough to beat their wives, or the girls married into a new village and couldn't get used to living with their in-laws. Others had sick children. When the women put their personal problems to me I always told them to revert back to the Bible because, if they took their grounding from the Scriptures, many could have the home they dreamed of having.'

The people's enthusiasm for God's Word never waned, even when they were in obvious distress. One day, Ron and Aggie sailed to an island devastated by Hurricane Bebe and were shocked to see the extent of the damage. The land had been stripped, leaving the inhabitants homeless and without food. Ron was almost ashamed to hold his usual meeting, and after the film show he stood up and blurted out an apology. 'I should have brought you a sack of rice, I didn't realise the situation here. I'm very sorry. I should have brought you something to eat, but all I can offer you is the Word of God.'

The Bible, however, was enough. As Ron finished talking, the crowd of some 300 people – the entire population of the island – gathered around the small Scripture display table. They bought almost everything! As he packed his equipment away at the end of the evening, Ron calculated that each family must have bought at least one Bible, a New Testament, and six or seven Scripture portions. He suddenly felt very humble in the face of such faith.

In April 1973 *Dayspring* set sail for Tuvalu, a remote part of the central Pacific which served as an American base during the Second World War. The nine islands in the group are all low-lying reef islands or coral atolls, and the Polynesian people rely heavily on foreign aid from Britain, Australia, and New Zealand. Despite their hard life, the islanders are extremely friendly and often spend their evenings singing and dancing in the village community hall.

On arrival, Ron and Aggie embarked on a hectic schedule, stopping for two or three days at each island. In addition to holding their usual Bible Society meetings, they met with Sunday school teachers, deacons, lay preachers and youth groups, and called on government officials, schools and hospitals. The Russell family were accompanied by two crew members, a Fijian from Savusavu and a Frenchman. The Fijian, a Roman Catholic, was an excellent sailor who spent days perched up on the mast, scanning the horizon for the smaller islands in the Tuvaluan group.

The Frenchman, however, was a problem. He was seasick during the entire five-day trip from Suva to Funafuti, Tuvalu's administration centre, and once on land his long black beard frightened the Tuvaluan people. Ron quietly asked him to shave it off as it was hindering the crew's relationship with the islanders, but he refused. When the Frenchman finally decided to return to Fiji by air, Ron was relieved. He explains, 'The whole idea of our work in these islands is to be available to the people, to adapt ourselves to their culture.' The Frenchman was not prepared to follow this golden rule. However, Ron later heard that he had returned to France where, minus his beard, he joined a Christian group dedicated to evangelism at sea. Perhaps he had finally learned his lesson!

Maika flew out to join the *Dayspring* team at Funafuti and they held numerous meetings among the islanders. Again, signs of Bebe's destruction were everywhere. Ships had been wrecked, thousands of coconut trees had fallen, and the people had been made homeless, yet they greeted their visitors with their usual cheerful manner. The people at the next port of call, Vaitupu Island, were just as welcoming. The Russells arrived in the middle of a joyous celebration to mark the centenary of the arrival of the original *Dayspring*! On seeing Ron and Aggie's yacht, the people started their merrymaking all over again, and days of singing and dancing followed. Maika spent hours talking to the islanders and by the time the crew left, they had distributed some 800 Scriptures.

In Kiribati (formerly the Gilbert Islands), the reception from the Micronesian population was quieter. The 33 coral islands are scattered over almost two million square miles of the central Pacific, and on one island the *Dayspring* crew found only twelve inhabitants. They were barely interested in the message brought by Ron and Maika. One man, however, a drunkard with a bad reputation, stood on the edge of the group. He listened as Ron told the story of his own conversion and testified to the power of Christ in his life. When Ron had finished, no one moved to buy any Scriptures and the group began to break up.

Suddenly, the outsider began, almost shyly, to move forward. He looked at the display and picked up the Gospel, then he turned to a Bible and read a few pages. 'How much?' he asked, pointing to a copy of the New Testament. Ron told him, and the man replied, 'I'll take it. I also want one of those . . . and that one . . .

and could I have some of these, please?' The man left with an armful of Scriptures and he read them throughout the night, squatting in his hut by the light of a kerosene lamp. As the dawn broke he was a changed man. Kneeling in the sand he said a silent prayer to God, thanking him for *Dayspring*'s visit and for the Good News of Jesus Christ.

In fact, despite its disappointing start, the trip to Kiribati turned out to be very successful. Ron went on to sell some sixty-four Bibles, and the Bible Society later sent another 1,250 for distribution throughout the island group.

During the voyage Ron was particularly impressed with Maika Bovoro, the government official who had given up his career to serve the Bible needs of the South Pacific. Maika, an excellent linguist, had first been called to the work because of an important Scripture translation project. Maurice Harvey, then Secretary of the New Zealand Bible Society's English-speaking agency in the Pacific, recalls, 'We first employed Maika as a translator of the Fijian New Testament. He had trained as an administrative officer for the government and was an expert in his language. We asked the government if they would give Maika leave of absence to work for the Bible Society but they refused – the country was on the eve of independence and he was just too valuable to them. However, it was important to translate the Word of God into the modern language of the Fijian people and so Maika eventually resigned and joined Bible Society.'

Maurice Harvey is now based in Reading, England, where he works as a photo-journalist for the United Bible Societies, and he has fond memories of Maika. 'He is the kind of fellow that you never hear a bad word about. He's such a lovable man, and spends himself in the service of other people – he is a real father-confessor.'

Ron quickly became aware of Maika's unique talent for communication. On one island the inhabitants were disturbed because the young pastors had been learning a new theology which discredited much of the Old Testament. They described the stories of Noah, Moses and others as nonsense, and the older people were confused. As soon as Maika realised what was happening, he stood before the assembled villagers and laid his faith on the line. 'The Word of God as it appears in the Bible is true. No ifs, no buts, no doubts, no watering down. The Bible is completely accurate and reliable.' His words were effective and restored the faith of the village. The next day, the islanders held a big ceremony in honour of the *Dayspring* team and gathered on the beach to wave goodbye to the bringers of Good News.

But the story did not end there. As Ron set sail, a fresh trade wind blew up so he made his way into a small bay on the other side of the island, where the crew laid out all anchors and battened down for the day. They sat in the saloon, drinking coffee and talking. Suddenly, they heard a faint voice above the elements and Ron went on deck to investigate. A small man was standing on the shore, waving and calling but his words were drowned by the wind. It was obvious that he wanted to come aboard so one of the crewmen went to collect him. Once inside the cabin, the islander told his story.

'I saw you there, Mr Bovoro. And you too, Mr Russell. I saw you over the heads of the people – the crowd pushed me to the back. I could sort of hear what you said, Mr Bovoro, but not much, only bits – they were good bits though, and I tried to push my way closer.'

Stopping for a moment, the man looked down at the floor and clasped his hands in front of him. 'I'm, well, a small man ... not too strong, though I can work as hard as the next man. Well, the crowd kept me back, I couldn't see and I couldn't hear. Then you left and I was sad. I watched you sail along the coast, and I could see the wind was giving you trouble. I started to follow but I couldn't keep up. I don't walk very fast either. Then someone said your boat was anchored here, so I walked across.'

Ron and Maika looked at the man in astonishment. The bay was at least six miles across rugged country from the village they had just left! It turned out that their unexpected visitor was a lay preacher who had been troubled by the young pastors and was seeking Christ. He spent the rest of the day in the cabin saloon, talking and studying the Bible, Ron remembers the man who reminded him of the New Testament Zacchaeus: 'Some hours later he emerged from the cabin and stood in the cockpit. The wind was strong but it didn't bother him, and he smiled as he left *Dayspring*. His journey across the island had been worthwhile, and he had found what he was looking for.'

The ministry was rewarding but it took its toll on Aggie. 'The boat never stops rolling and you are sort of in a prison – when you want to do some sewing you can't hold the needle properly, when you want to write, you can't.' She has vivid memories of those early voyages. The Russells would carry as many Scriptures as possible on board their small boat, with boxes of Bibles packed in the shower, or used as seats until they reached their destination, Aggie comments, 'For a married couple there was no privacy. We carried pastors, we carried translators, we carried guides,

83

People were in and out and June-Ann was crying, wanting to get this and that!'

It was, and still is, extremely tiring work, as Ron explains. 'Quite often we have to anchor on the windward side of islands because that's where the villages are. Normally yachtsmen go into a quiet, nice anchorage, get in their bunks and recover. But we can't. The people are waiting for us.'

One day the Russells moored alongside a small coastal village. The setting was idyllic, near a beach fringed with coconut trees. 'All right, Ron,' Aggie said, 'put your head down for an hour's sleep. June-Ann and I will have a shower, it's so hot and sticky.' However, as Ron made his way to the cabin he noticed that people were already gathering on the beach, watching the boat. Aggie noticed, too. 'Don't worry, just rest, you're so tired.' She began to prepare things for the meeting ahead – the fifteenth in less than three weeks – and then she noticed canoes putting out from the shore. They were full of children.

Soon there were a dozen small vessels alongside *Dayspring* and the children, thinking the Russells were tourists were clamouring for attention. 'Nice shells. Look. 'You buy?'

Aggie leaned over the railing. 'Shhh. We're not tourists, we're from the Bible Society. We bring the Word of God.' The children began to talk among themselves and one boy stood up, reaching towards Aggie with a large white shell. 'You take.' Aggie told him to wait a moment and disappeared into the cabin. She returned with some brightly coloured Scripture selections. 'Here, take these. They're in your language. The Bible Society translated them so you could read them yourselves. Here.' She passed them down to outstretched hands. The children chattered excitedly and paddled back to the beach.

Aggie was grateful for a few moments of peace – until she realised that an even larger group was gathering on the beach and more children were jumping into canoes and making their way to *Dayspring*. 'Oh no,' she groaned, and called out, 'Wait. Just wait. We'll be coming ashore later with plenty of books, and we'll show films tonight.' Aggie disappeared into the cabin, hoping to have a shower and prepare Ron's clothes, but the children had reached the boat and she could feel the eyes staring through the portholes.

Ron was not able to rest. In no time at all, the village pastor set out in his own canoe and invited the Russells ashore. They had no choice but to accept, and made their way wearily to the reception awaiting them. It was ten hours before they were finally able to return to the boat, and a much needed rest.

The reception was not always as enthusiastic, even when attendance was high. At one gathering over 900 people were packed into the local church. They had come from all around, some walking as many as ten miles to hear the message from the *Dayspring*. Nevertheless, once the meeting was over the people filed out, not even glancing at the Scripture display. Ron was disappointed. 'This is heartbreaking, Aggie. All those people and we didn't touch them. We failed here. I've sailed for three days for this.'

Aggie was beginning to feel the strain. 'Ron, it makes me wonder why we are doing this. Why have we come this long way, done all this work? What is the use of it all? I could have shaken some of those people. I understood what some of them said in their language – you didn't. It was sarcastic! Let's give it all up. Let's go!'

Ron looked at his wife. 'No, Aggie. God has allowed us to come here. He has allowed His Word to be made available. Remember the times when people have crowded nine and ten deep around the table, pressing so we could hardly breathe. And remember all the people who have come to know Christ because of the Bibles we have distributed.'

Aggie knew Ron was right. She looked up and said, 'Well, Lord, this is where you want us and you have compassion for all types of people. We'll carry on.'

When Ron and Aggie returned to Auckland in May 1974 they were promptly reprimanded, for the people from their church had discovered that they were not eating properly. The church decided to give the couple a freezer to run off the engine, so that fruit and vegetables would always be available on long voyages. There were other gifts. One church member donated a new Genoa sail, some gave small items of equipment, still more gave money so that *Dayspring* could be completely re-sprayed.

Ron embarked on a short tour of New Zealand to tell the people of his ministry in the South Seas and, again, the gifts kept coming. One day he drove to a small town to address a tiny meeting and when he finished speaking a woman approached him. She had been at the previous evening's gathering, and she said, 'This morning, my husband and I were holding our devotions as usual, and I believe the Lord spoke to us. He wants us to give our milk cheque to you for your wonderful work. So I drove right across here to present it to you.' She duly handed the cheque to Ron.

Shortly after, Ron set sail for the Polynesian islands of Western Samoa. He had arranged to meet up with Maika in the capital of Apia, on the island of Upolu, before travelling on to the Tokelau Islands some 300 miles north. The people had no Bible in their own language and Maika wanted to investigate the possibility of starting translation work, On the way, *Dayspring* ran into a gale. It was the middle of the night and Ron's Danish crewmate, Oscar Jorgensen, was asleep. Ron was at the helm and he soon found himself struggling against the weather as the waves crashed over the boat. Suddenly the engine oil pipe burst, covering the cockpit with oil. Slipping and sliding, Ron tried to steer and fix the problem at the same time, but then the steering broke! A pin had sheared through on the steering shaft and Ron had no spare, so he decided to improvise with a piece of wire and some metal. As dawn broke, the weather improved and Oscar returned to deck, unaware of the traumatic night Ron had endured alone. To his relief, the remainder of the voyage was uneventful.

After a short break in Apia, *Dayspring* made her way to the three atolls in the Tokelaus group. Atafu, Fakaofo, and Nukunonu are so remote that they can usually only be reached by a steamer which makes the journey every three months, stopping briefly to unload cargo and passengers. Dr Ray Rickards, a United Bible Societies (UBS) translation consultant, joined Ron and his crew for this journey. He had never done any yachting before and he wrote of his experiences: 'After three days and two nights, the *Dayspring* sighted Atafu, the most northerly of the atolls. That sighting will be hard to forget. I'd been at the helm since two a.m. and had been relieved by Maika at about four o'clock. Just as dawn was breaking, Maika suddenly shouted excitedly, bringing all hands on deck. There, in the early tropical morning light, was a small atoll not more than a couple of miles straight ahead. Ron had calculated we'd reach it at that time, and he was dead on. The old sextant had proved right again!'

The crew made their way to the other side of the islet, and anchored at a point near the entrance to the lagoon, By this time, the islanders had spotted their visitors, and were waving and shouting in great excitement. Some made their way to *Dayspring* in small boats. 'The first to greet us was the Rev. Kuata Pue, Congregational pastor of the six hundred inhabitants of the islet. Stepping down from the *Dayspring* into the bobbing boats, we were conveyed expertly through the narrow opening in the reef into the quiet waters of a small artificial harbour. As we walked from the jetty to the village, friendly faces ranked our pathway, and our hands were wrung fervently and frequently. This welcome on Atafu continued unabated. For the 36 hours we were there, the islanders did everything imaginable for our enjoyment and comfort.'

There was only one village at Atafu, but it was spotlessly clean. The houses, or 'fales', were constructed of local timber, with walls and roofs of platted pandanus, and the *Dayspring* team held several meetings at the 'fale fono', or meeting house. Here they showed films and sold English and Samoan Scriptures, and discussions on the Tokelauan Bible were also fruitful. A small committee was appointed and Pastor Kuata Pue was chosen to produce the first drafts of the translation. As Ron and the others made their way back to *Dayspring* they were showered with parting gifts of mats, baskets, fruit and vegetables. They were even given money for Bible Society work, despite the fact that the community did not have a cash economy.

The next port of call was Nukunonu, some 57 miles south of Atafu and the largest atoll in the group. Travelling through the night, Ron had trouble in finding a safe anchorage. He decided to stay on board while Maika and Dr Rickards went ashore and watched as the islanders came to fetch them. The only means of transportation, a large long-boat, had to be navigated through the narrow opening in the reef at just the right moment, on the crest of a suitable wave. There was one close shave when the long-boat suddenly crashed against the left-hand side of the passage, tilting the boat dangerously. Maika and the others thought they would all be tossed into the foaming surf, but in an instant several of the strong oarsmen had jumped over the side. Grasping a rope thrown out from the shallower water, which they secured to the bow, the men pulled the boat to safety inside the reef. The passage was a particularly tricky one. Only two years later one of the islanders was killed while taking another boat through the same narrow area.

Once on dry land, the Bible Society representatives received a warm welcome from the Roman Catholic islanders, who were ministered to by Father Tuvia, a Samoan. Maika and Dr Rickards quickly set up a translation committee and chose a young school teacher, Tominika Tuia, to produce the first drafts for part of the Tokelauan Bible project. When they returned to *Dayspring* Ron sailed 40 miles south, to the third atoll of Fakaofo, where he accompanied the team ashore. The inhabitants, a mixture of Congregationalists and Roman Catholics, greeted each man with a coconut shell which contained a delicious porridge. The gift was a symbol of Christian fellowship, and far more appealing than the old custom of greeting newcomers with spears!

Because the *Dayspring* had arrived at a weekend, the crew were able to worship in one of the European-style churches built by the early missionaries. 'The women wore hats platted from pandanus leaves,' Ron recalls, 'and were segregated from the men. There was no nonsense from the younger members of the congregation as the deacons kept their eye on them and were ready with long sticks to correct any who misbehaved!'

The farewell ceremony took place in pouring rain,

but this did not spoil the singing, dancing and humorous sketches which transcended all language barriers. Just as the crew were preparing to leave, the Fainuku, the chief councillor of the village, presented Maika with even more money. This brought the total donation from the Tokelau Islands to $2,500 – an enormous amount for an area with just over one and a half thousand inhabitants.

Ron's latest voyage had been a successful one, and, after two years afloat he was beginning to realise the importance of the *Dayspring* ministry. He was really impressed with Maika and the islanders, but Dr Rickards was equally impressed with the English sailor who was becoming a significant force in the South Seas. After the trip to the Tokelaus, Dr Rickards wrote, 'I couldn't help but develop a deep admiration for Ron Russell as a person and sailor. His navigational skill and cheerful temperament, his tirelessness and capacity for sustained hard work, and, most of all, his dedication to the cause of spreading the Good News of Jesus Christ, are beyond praise. Like Maika, I was grateful the Lord had sent Ron and the *Dayspring* to serve Him through the Bible Society in the South Pacific. Without this Christian sailor and his boat, the work the Society is committed to would be seriously impaired.'

6. New Horizons

'Look,' Ron said, 'I can't match you people. All I can say is one thing. When you put that book of philosophy down, you'll pick up another one, and when another book is written, you'll pick that up. But this Bible will never move! It will be the same in a hundred years. The Bible will always be the same and it is the only plumbline or yardstick you can have. It's no good me debating philosophy with you two, I'm beaten.'

Ron was on board a yacht owned by Larry Reed and his wife, a middle-aged couple who were 'into philosophy'. Larry, an American, was the son of a pastor but he had turned away from Christianity so, when Ron arrived and started to talk about God, he and his wife jumped on their visitor with gusto. The discussion was a good-humoured one and Ron stayed for more than an hour. Larry's wife, was intrigued by his arguments, bought a New Testament, and shortly after this first meeting she also purchased a modern version of the Bible.

The weeks passed and Ron and Aggie prepared for yet another voyage to the Pacific islands. Shortly before they were due to sail, Aggie told Ron to take Larry a Bible. Ron was a bit apprehensive, but he made his way to the Reed's yacht and said, 'Larry, would you please accept this Word of God before you go?'

Ron was astounded when Larry replied, 'Well, thank you, Ron. I really appreciate that!'

When the Russells met the couple again a few days later, Aggie was convinced that Larry's wife was on the verge of becoming a Christian. She remembers, 'She had changed her whole attitude and her husband had started reading the Bible.' They were to hear more from the Reeds in the years to come.

Ron's ministry to yachties was fruitful. At every large port there were always other boats moored nearby, and it was easy to start friendships. Ron comments, 'They all know the "Bible boat". There's probably about 700 yachts sailing around the world at any one time and, because of radio communications, *Dayspring* is being mentioned constantly. In fact, it's quite amusing to see a boat come into the bay and then go out again because the crew has seen us. But they don't know us, we're really not like that at all. If we do happen to meet a boat, we like to share with the people on board, but, if spiritual things don't come up, we just like to enjoy their company. But it is exciting from time to time, because we can really minister to some of the yachtsmen who, I believe, understand God because of the very nature of what they do, sailing out on the ocean.'

In the autumn of 1974 Ron and Aggie set sail for a small island near Vanua Levu. They arrived late in the afternoon and after the film show the villagers asked the couple to stay and teach them more about the Bible. They were still deep in conversation at two o'clock in the afternoon the following day. Ron knew he should be on his way but the islanders would have none of it. They had prepared a feast for the crew and the *Dayspring* team had no choice but to stay. Nevertheless, as the hours slipped away Ron began to

94

worry and told his hosts, 'Look, we must get away.' He gestured towards a peninsula some five miles off the mainland. 'I promised the school over there that I'd come and show a film tonight. This is the last day the children will be around because the school holidays start tomorrow.' Although Ron loved the friendly culture of the Pacific, sometimes the laid-back attitude could be frustrating, especially for someone from the time-conscious Western world.

His impatience grew as the villagers, unimpressed by the note of urgency in his voice, told him, 'Plenty of time'.

It was late in the afternoon before Ron finally found himself back on *Dayspring*. It was only an hour's run to his destination, but it was a tricky journey, for there were several reefs on the way and he did not want to navigate when the sun was too far down. Then a canoe rowed out from the village. The chief, a charming, blind, white-haired old man, wanted the crew to return to shore so that he could make a presentation. Ron was unsure what to do – he didn't want to offend the people who had been so hospitable but he could not disappoint the children either. He told the head spokesman, 'Look, I can't come. We're going to miss out if we don't sail now.' The islander pleaded again, so Ron relented, praying that he had not let himself in for a long Fijian ceremony. His misgivings were well-founded, for the presentation went on for some time and the chief sat, sombre and cross-legged, going slowly through the proceedings. Ron was frantic, the hours were slipping away and the sun was dropping lower in the sky.

Finally, at a tactfully appropriate moment, he made his move. 'We must go, because the sun is going down. We have to get through the channel and our boat is not very fast.' The villagers wanted the

Dayspring crew to stay for the night and one of them warned, 'You'd better be careful of the reefs.'

The chief added, 'If you can't make it, there's a little island just two miles away, clear of all the danger, and you can rest there.'

The Russells made their way to the dinghy and cast off, but by the time they reached *Dayspring* the sun was very low and visibility was poor. Ron yanked the anchor up and decided to take a chance – instead of following the main channel where the markers were, he could save time by cutting across inside the reef. He put the engine on full speed. His crewman, Joe Kanacagi, a young Fijian from Savusavu, was at the mast top as lookout, and Aggie was at the bow, peering ahead and down. Ron looked at his charts and estimated he had plenty of water and clearance over the reef, but he had forgotten one thing – the chart was an old one.

Aggie was watching carefully and all seemed to go well, until suddenly *Dayspring* hit something! The boat jarred, bounced heavily into the air, and slid into deep water. The keel had run into the very end of the long, narrow reef. Nobody was hurt but everyone was shaken, so Ron decided to head for the little island mentioned by the chief. When he inspected the hull, he could see that it wasn't holed, although a large chunk of cement had been taken from the keel. The hammering had also broken the pipes to the freezer but the boat was still seaworthy. Ron gave a prayer of thanks. God was looking after his boat and, despite the delays, the children saw the films after all.

The constant voyages tired Aggie, so when Ron embarked on a seven-week trip to the Lau Islands in August 1975, she stayed behind with June-Ann. Ron had always wanted to visit the Lau group, and an earlier trip had been cut short by bad weather, but he had some misgivings. The islands had a bad reputation amongst sailors because they were ocean islands, with no large areas of land or other islands to act as windbreaks, and the seas could be very rough. But the weather was good when Ron set sail for the group's most southern island of Ono-i-Lau, accompanied by Joe Kanacagi and Pauliaski Rokomatu, the Assistant Director of Evangelism in the Methodist Church.

It was a clear and bright morning when land came into view, but first Ron had to navigate a wide reef across the entrance to the harbour. Two prominent rocks marked a clear passage but on entry Ron could sense that something was wrong. He had taken a false passage and the current swept *Dayspring* onto the reef. Ron was trapped and his boat was in danger of being pounded to pieces. He remembers, 'I won't try to describe the agony of the next half hour, as *Dayspring* shuddered with waves pounding over her. I was overcome with hopelessness and a sense of failure. All we could do was cry out to the Lord!'

Then he had an idea. If he lightened the load by rowing across the lagoon with the fuel, water and Bibles, *Dayspring* might be able to come off the reef with the next tide. Ron prayed quietly as he climbed into the dinghy, but before he could sit down a great swell rolled over the reef, lifting the boat and carrying her forward.

Ron held tight to the side as she skidded across the reef in a series of bumps, before settling in the lagoon. He clambered back on board and weaved the boat through the coral heads. His prayers had been answered and *Dayspring* was safe. Once at Ono-i-Lau, one of the young village chiefs swam out under the boat to check for damage. The underside of the keel had broken away to the first layer of the steel rod, the fillings round one of the bolts had broken off, and *Dayspring* had a slight leak, but all these things were minor and could be patched up.

Although the boat had survived with only superficial damage, Ron had hurt his back and was in considerable pain. Nevertheless, he stayed in the Lau group for six weeks, holding forty meetings on some twenty islands and receiving the full Fijian welcome at each. He managed to distribute 600 Bibles, 1,200 New Testaments, and thousands of Scripture portions and selections. By September 1975, Maika was reporting to the UBS, 'Stocks are very low at the headquarters of the Bible Society in the South Pacific.' *Dayspring* was proving her worth!

Ron has many memories of this tour, and one island in particular made a deep impression on him, Naitauba was owned by American film and TV star Raymond Burr – known to millions as Perry Mason or 'Ironside' – and the actor ran a copra plantation there. A Methodist leader ministered to the workers and Ron was given permission to hold a meeting. Some 150 people attended and after Ron had shown the films, Rokomatu stood up and invited them to give their lives to Christ. The response was overwhelming. Almost every young person on the island came forward. Rokomatu counselled each of them and Ron also spoke to many. He remembers, 'I'm convinced the conversions were genuine. There was a reality behind it.'

The young islanders bought almost everything on the Scripture table, and it was very late by the time they finally dispersed. As Ron and his crew walked towards their hut, the chief suddenly appeared and told them, 'The young people are so grateful for your visit and they've got together and made up some special songs in honour of *Dayspring*.'

The men accompanied the chief onto the verandah and were suddenly confronted with over forty people, gathered together on the sand at the front of the hut. Slowly the islanders began to sing and their voices soon filled the tropical evening air. Ron comments, 'For me, it was one of the most moving moments of the ministry and emotion welled up inside me. It was a long way from Auckland and the shed in which *Dayspring* had slowly taken shape. As I listened to the singing of the young people, I felt the strength of their faith, and I knew that the long hours of lonely labour had all been worthwhile!'

Towards the end of the voyage Ron decided to visit another beautiful plantation island owned by a Mr Breden, a man notorious for his lack of hospitality. Worried that his labourers would be enticed away by outsiders, Breden would allow no visitors to his South Pacific paradise. However, the island was on course so Ron sent him a telegram, explaining that he was a Bible Society representative and would be arriving shortly.

Once ashore Ron telephoned Breden, who reluctantly agreed to meet him, and as the two men faced each other on the wharf Breden spoke first. 'What do you people want? Who are the Bible Society?' Ron told him, but Breden replied, 'All these people are Methodists, they don't need Bibles.'

Ron refused to give up: 'That's all right. We help all churches. We've just come to explain the work of the Society, and to share what we do with them. We have these Scriptures available in case some of them want to look into the Word of God.'

Breden was stubborn. He told Ron that the workers never held meetings on work days, and that no transport would be available until much later in the day. Ron persisted: 'Would you give me permission to bring my Bibles and projector and films to the wharf? We'll wait patiently until a truck is available, no matter what the time is. I'm sure the people will be happy about this.'

Breden gave in. 'All right, have your own way. You bring your Bibles.' With that, he drove his Land-Rover back to the top of the hill, and Ron never saw him again. However, permission had been granted and, by four-thirty the *Dayspring* team had their equipment ready. A truck arrived at five and the welcome at the plantation was astounding. The meeting hall was crowded and the workers, half Fijians, half Indians, were delighted to see their Bible Society representatives. They had never witnessed anything like it before and they took advantage of this unique opportunity to purchase Scriptures. When Ron sailed away the next morning he was glad he had found the courage to persevere with his awkward customer, and that God had sent him to the island nobody was allowed to visit.

Once back in Suva, Ron wrote a newsletter to his Christian friends. 'It's been seven gruelling weeks and the Skipper has come home with a strained back and a very tired team. It does cost a little to see Christ in action, but what's that compared with the privilege of being in the battle, and claiming His inevitable victory? God has been extra good to us.' It had been an eventful year – particularly for the Bible Society in the South Pacific. Because of Maika's successful administration, the Society gained independence from New Zealand in November 1975. It was now well on its way to becoming a national Bible Society within the United Bible Societies' family and, from humble beginnings, the workforce grew to include an Accountant/Office Manager, a Production and Supply Consultant, a Translations Consultant, and an Advisory Committee.

Within a few short months, Ron was at sea again. It was April 1976 and the Russell family were about to embark on a six months' tour of duty through Vanuatu, the Solomon Islands, New Caledonia, and the Loyalty Islands. They were accompanied by Mase Teoneo, a young Tuvaluan raised in Fiji, who had been employed for several years as a storeman and packer for the Bible Society. When invited to join the *Dayspring* team, Mase had given up his job in faith, confident that the Lord would provide for his material needs. He became a valued member of the crew and a life-long friend of the Russells.

The first port of call, Vanuatu, was originally named the New Hebrides because the local mountain ranges reminded Captain Cook of Scotland. The string of lush tropical islands form part of a chain of volcanic activity stretching from New Zealand through to the New Guinea islands. Ron headed for the centre of the group, the island of Efate, and docked in the cosmopolitan capital of Port Vila, known for its beautiful waterfalls. It is home to over 14,000 people, and the demand for Bibles was high. Ron and Aggie sold all the Scriptures on board as well as stocks that had been lying in the local bookshop. They had to fly in extra supplies from Suva before continuing with the tour.

As they travelled on to the larger islands of Malekula and Espiritu Santo the weather was not always kind. 'Buffeted by strong trade winds,' Ron remembers, 'it was tough going but we were able to reach many island villages and mission stations. The winds from the south-east forced us to turn back to shelter from some of the nastiest seas we'd ever experienced. The second trip was even more rugged and we were constantly beaten up as we went from island to island.'

Aggie realised that journeys on land could be just as perilous when *Dayspring* arrived at the picturesque island of Aoba, famous for its extinct crater and warm-water lake. She and Ron decided to visit the Diocesan Training Centre at Torgill to see Derek Rawcliffe, the Anglican Bishop of Vanuatu, who was a keen Bible Society supporter. However, the centre was situated in a harbour by the sunken crater, and to reach it the Russells had to make their way across a steep hill. They got to their destination safely enough but it was late at night when they set out on the return journey. The transport was unusual – an open trailer pulled behind a mission tractor – and the driver's only source of light was from a small hand torch. The road left much to be desired and, to make matters worse, the rain fell in torrents. Before long Aggie was at her wit's end and, in her own inimitable way, she made her feelings very plain to both Ron and the driver! Looking back, she laughs, 'Being soaked to the skin was bad enough, but to be pulled along over a bumpy track, not knowing whether we would all soon plunge to our deaths over a cliff in the dark, was the last straw. I told Ron, "Never again!"'

Resilient as ever, Aggie soon recovered and she and Ron travelled on to the town of Duindui to meet Keith and Shirley Ludgater, who had a daughter the same age as June-Ann. The couple were both ordained Church of Christ ministers and Keith had been working with fellow missionary Dorothy Dewar to translate the New Testament and some Scripture selections into the local language. A few months after Ron and Aggie's visit the Ludgaters returned to Australia to take up a new ministry, and passing through the Bible Society offices in Suva, Keith was thrilled to see the first batch of New Reader booklets that he and Dorothy had translated.

From Vanuatu, Ron and Aggie journeyed north to the scattered chain of islands known as the Solomons, Santa Cruz, Santa Ana, San Cristobal, and Honiara on Guadalcanal received their Spanish names from the sixteenth-century explorer Alvaro de Mendana de Neyra. Thinking they were part of a great southern continent he named the group Solomon, after the rich biblical king, to entice his fellow countrymen to colonise them. Today, the Melanesian inhabitants of this generally mountainous area are fond of artistic body ornaments and live in bamboo and thatch homes fronted by ornate wood carvings. Almost 90 per cent of the people rely on a subsistence economy, and the traditional copra export has recently been supplemented by oil palm and rice plantations.

En route, Ron decided to visit one small group which lived in almost Stone Age conditions for many years. He remembers, 'Resting in a small cove in Motolava, the trade wind humming in the rigging, we prayed that the Lord would show us His will regarding a tiny island, perhaps the remotest in the Pacific. It meant going 200 miles off our course but on the next day, for the first time in many months, the trade wind ceased to blow and, with a light south-westerly wind, we sailed for Tikopia.' Ron was anxious to share his faith with the Polynesians at this most southerly point but he was disappointed. Many societies in the outlying islands still practise ancestor or shark worship, and the people of Tikopia had revived many non-Christian customs from the past. The *Dayspring* team left the area some five days later feeling that they had accomplished nothing.

To make matters worse, the visit was particularly traumatic for June-Ann, as Ron explains: 'She was a very sheltered girl and I think the island of Tikopia was perhaps a turning point for her. When she went ashore there were about thirty children rushing around her – she was quite young and just like a little china doll – they had never seen anyone quite like it. They pawed her and, although they didn't do any harm, June-Ann was so frightened. After that, she just shied away from crowds.'

Aggie continues, 'It was very hard for me to get June-Ann to go ashore after Tikopia. As soon as we approached land she would cry to me, "Oh Mummy, please ask Daddy if I cannot go ashore today, I'm so frightened." Often, Ron and I had to be really strict and force her to go with us. We just pray that she will get over some of the hurts, as we believe that we were where God wanted us to be at that time in her life.'

On arrival at Honiara, the capital of the Solomons and a colourful city of wide lawns, tulips and streets lined with fig and palm trees, the Russell family were given a warm welcome. The local branch of the Bible Society was run by missionary-wife Edna Nash, and Ron remembers, 'We were able to hold many meetings and experienced wonderful fellowship there. For most of the time the hunger for Scriptures and Christian literature was very real.'

The islanders boast almost 100 native languages, but the majority speak Solomon Island Pijin. Just a year after Ron and Aggie's visit, Maika Bovoro returned to Honiara for a very special ceremony, the presentation of the Gospel of Mark in that language. It was the first book of the Bible ever to be translated into the local Pijin and Maika commented, 'To us in the Bible Society and the churches our mandate is clear. The words that our God spoke long ago to the Hebrew world in Hebrew and to the Greek world in Greek must be put into the Solomon Island Pidgin in order that the world of Solomon Island Pidgin might understand Him . . . We hope that as people hear the

104

Gospel being read today, they will come to appreciate its beauty and simplicity and will take it as the beginning of a Bible that can be truly their own.'

Ron left Aggie and June-Ann in Honiara while he and Mase travelled to New Caledonia, a French overseas territory and one of the world's largest producers of nickel. The area is known for its natural beauty – turquoise-green waters, dazzling sandy beaches, coconut palms and forests of wild orchids and ferns. The main island is one of the largest in the South Pacific, and the second greatest barrier reef in the world flanks the west coast. Along the east coast, tribes live in traditional round houses with conical roofs which have changed little since the days of Captain Cook. The capital city of Noumea, the Paris of the South Pacific, bears a strong French influence and is home to over 60,000 people of mostly Melanesian and European descent.

Once in Noumea, Ron realised that he would need a translator, for the largely Roman Catholic community was 90 per cent French-speaking. God always seemed to provide the right man at the right time and, sure enough, he was offered the services of a young Frenchman, Patrick Giraudel. Patrick, the pastor of the Assemblies of God Church, was on a two months' vacation and he provided valuable assistance throughout Ron's stay. By this time Maika had also arrived on the scene, and the men joined forces with Peter and Jean Compton, a New Zealand couple who ran a bookshop called Les Flambeaux in the town. A trade fair provided the ideal setting for a Bible Society display, as Ron remembers: 'There we were, in the middle of the square, distributing the "Sermon on the Mount" in French from our stall. Maika and Patrick helped to distribute 2,000 Scripture selections and portions and it was simply wonderful to sit back and see God in action.' Such was the support for the Bible Society that, while Ron was in Noumea, a working committee was formed to set up a local branch.

Eventually Aggie and June-Ann flew out to meet Ron and the family spent another five weeks in New Caledonian waters, visiting the Melanesian Loyalty Islands and filming for the Bible Society of Australia before finally returning to New Zealand in late November. Ron remembers, 'Aggie flew back, while Mase, another crew member Robert Belmont, and myself set sail for home. As soon as we got outside the harbour the wind shifted completely. We were expecting a south-easterly for at least 500 miles, but the wind changed to the north-west and we had an incredibly-fast passage back to Auckland. In fact, we were so fast that we beat Aggie and she was very surprised to find Mase at the airport – she didn't even recognise me as I was dressed up in dark glasses and an overcoat and it was quite hilarious!' This latest voyage had lasted seven long months and the Russells took a well-earned rest at a little cottage in a Christian beach camp in Willow Park, Auckland.

In February 1977, Ron wrote another newsletter. 'Now that we have completed a month's work using *Dayspring* in the annual Water Weeks, she's ready to be hauled out and refitted for a further five years in the South Pacific. She's had five years of really hard work and there is much to be done to bring her up to standard. Rigging, sails, and engine will need renewing and overhauling, besides paint work inside and out.' Privately, Ron and Aggie were beginning to wonder if *Dayspring* really was big enough for the expanding opportunities and challenges in the South Pacific. They looked at one or two new boats until, through a friend, they came across a 55-foot ferro-cement sailer, the *Innisfree*.

Aggie recalls, 'When I looked at this boat I said: "This is the one for us, the Lord's going to give us this boat!" We were told the price and I really liked the layout. I knew that God's work could be accomplished in such a craft and we felt it was time to have a bigger boat.'

Ron continues, 'Marie, the owner's wife, was astounded when Aggie, baring her soul as always, blurted out, "This is the boat that God wants for the work." But I had reservations. My first impression was fear because it was so big – from 38 to 55 feet – and I thought, no, this can't be the one. But I realised that it had so much room that it would be absolutely ideal. At that time it seemed impossible that we could have it because, although we had *Dayspring*, we had very few funds.'

The Russells decided to put the project on ice because they had other things on their mind for the coming year. Ron wrote to friends, 'We are convinced that God would have us in England to see my family and share with interested folk of Bible Society, the Torchbearers, and other Christian groups, the work in the South Pacific.' 'Ron hadn't seen his mother for sixteen years,' Aggie points out, 'and I had never been to England – to us the possibility of going there seemed just a dream. We only had two thousand dollars and we had to pay half-fare for June-Ann, who was about seven or eight at the time. But then the Lord provided the means in a miraculous way – He opened up doors in every area. Through a gift, we were able to put *Dayspring* into a marina and we found the money for our fare – we made a firm booking and left for England on 23 March 1977.'

On the way to Britain Ron and Aggie made a detour to Macau, in Portuguese Hong Kong, where Aggie's aunt now lived, Aggie had often heard her father speak about his sister, who had cared for the family when his mother had died. He used to write to her occasionally and he had given Aggie her address but, unknown to him, it was twenty-five years old!

Once in Kowloon the Russells boarded the ferry to Macau but they were in a strange land and hopelessly lost, so Aggie decided to ask a man standing nearby if he knew the area. He told her, 'When we get to Macau, you will follow me, and I will do my best to find this address for you.' As soon as they arrived at their destination, Ron and Aggie queued up to get their passports stamped but, suddenly they were ushered to the front of the line and treated as VIPs. The couple knew nothing about their guide, but when they emerged onto the street, he led them to a large Mercedes-Benz with a chauffeur standing at the door.

Sitting next to the chauffeur, the man began to speak into a walkie-talkie. Ron and Aggie could understand nothing of what he was saying, who he was, or where they were going. When they finally arrived at the address, they were told that the family had moved, but then Aggie remembered that her cousin, Chang Tack, worked at the post office. On arrival the man told the Russells, 'I have to leave you here but please use my car and call me if you are stuck.' He left his card and Aggie suddenly realised that he was a most unusual 'Good Samaritan'. 'The card said that he was the Vice-President of the Casino – can you believe that! We thought it was very comical, missionaries meeting gamblers, but it was an experience and it was lovely of him to offer his kind services.'

The post office staff told the Russells that Chang Tack was at lunch, but they telephoned him and within a few minutes he arrived with a taxi to take his long-lost cousin home. Aggie recalls, 'We went down winding alleyways and into this quite slummish area, full of people and dogs, it was like something out of a picture book, it was fantastic. We eventually walked up into a very crooked and tumbling down old shack where my auntie was sitting with six Chinese ladies. Someone told me that she was a faith healer, that these people had brought their herbs and incense. She heard Chang Tack say who I was and she couldn't come out quickly enough! She couldn't do enough for us and it was a day of great rejoicing. We couldn't converse, so Chang Tack had to interpret, but it was a wonderful day – we rode rickshaws and she took us to the top of the Casino where she gave us the most fabulous Chinese meal.'

The family reunions far from over, Ron and Aggie caught the plane to England, but, as they neared their destination the 'prodigal son' began to feel nervous. When he had first left England Ron had been an atheist and an adventurer, something of a black sheep in the family. During the intervening years, however, three incredible things had happened to him: besides sailing halfway around the world, he now had a Fijian-Chinese wife and a daughter, and he was a Christian. Ron comments, 'I remember writing and getting no letters back at all, so we were really nervous when we touched down at Heathrow Airport. But, when we walked through Customs, there was the whole family – the plane had been delayed seven hours and it was eleven o'clock at night but they had waited all that time to greet us – it was absolutely marvellous.'

Knowing they would be spending a considerable amount of time in England with Ron's mother, the Russells made themselves available to the Bible

Society there. The staff planned a full itinerary of speaking engagements and the reception at churches throughout the country was overwhelming. 'We were just bowled over by the kindness and enthusiasm we found everywhere,' Ron recalls. 'We travelled to little villages, to cathedrals, to every type of venue one can possibly think of.' One of the early meetings was held in a Roman Catholic convent on a dark and stormy night. Ron spoke to some thirty people about *Dayspring*'s work and the need to replace her with a larger vessel. 'At the end of the evening, this dear old fellow came up and said: "I believe absolutely that you should have this bigger boat and here is something towards it." He gave me £500, a sizeable amount of money in those days, and that was the first of many gifts we received, We really believed the Lord was going to provide the other £20,000 for us to purchase the boat we had seen.'

Despite his wealth of experience in public speaking, Ron had his first pangs of 'stage fright' during the tour. 'On one occasion we went to a typical tenth-century church, in a village outside Wolverhampton, which was packed with around 300 ladies. I had to climb up this spiral staircase to get to the pulpit but it was built the wrong way round and, when I got up there, everything began to wobble. I mentioned something about being up the mast on a stormy day, and everybody roared with laughter – I was very grateful that the ice had been broken and we had a very good meeting.'

From there, the Russells were rushed across the infamous Spaghetti Junction on the motorway in Birmingham to attend a meeting at the Town Hall. They were late and their host, a Mr Blanch, was relieved to see them. Ron describes the occasion: 'It was the most incredible meeting I have ever had in my life. There must have been at least forty "dog collars" all looking at me, plus archbishops on either side, and there we were in the Lord Mayor's Chambers. Mr Blanch stood up and said, "Look, we're going to dispose with all the minutes and everything else and let this sailor "swing the lamp". I've asked him to tell us lots of stories about the South Pacific. They all made me feel totally relaxed, and I could see the delight on their faces when I told them the stories about the Bible reaching the islands and changing the lives of the people there. It was really great!'

From the outset of the tour, Ron knew that interest in the South Pacific would be high. He explains, 'It was from England that the early missionaries went to the South Pacific and really risked their lives. One of the earlier *Dayspring*s took the Good News round the islands and played a vital part in spreading Christianity, and there's still a vital interest in this.'

Aggie was very impressed. 'What fascinated me was the interest of the older folks – the people who usually have a little bring-and-buy stall at local church events – who had supported the Bible Society nearly all their lives. Some even had great-grand-parents and grandparents who had been supporters. The islanders couldn't purchase their heavily subsi-dised Bibles without the support of these elderly people. That's the thing that really encouraged me to go on distributing Scriptures in the Pacific, the enthusiasm of the folks in England.'

The tour was a tremendous success, and the trip back to New Zealand was an eventful one. Ron and Aggie had to return home via the United States, the cheapest route to New Zealand, and this gave them an opportunity to visit the Capernwray centre in Colorado. There was also an exciting diversion for June-Ann. 'We wanted to take June-Ann to Disneyland,' Aggi remembers, 'but we were very short of funds and were trying to keep as much money as we could for the boat – we channelled all the gifts we received towards the *Dayspring II* project. Then, out of the blue, an American family sent us a cheque with the instructions: "You're to spend all this on Disneyland!"'

Another friend in Los Angeles provided the Russells with an entrance ticket for the different rides, so they had enough to buy sweets and souvenirs – it was a wonderful trip. Aggie also fulfilled a life-long ambition. 'I had always wanted to see Hawaii and I said to Ron: "Oh, couldn't we divert to Honolulu? I just want to see Honolulu before I die!" Some dear friends in Wellington paid for the extra fare to divert to Hawaii and also offered us a condominium, so the Lord really did provide in a wonderful way.'

The holiday of a lifetime over, the Russell family arrived back in Auckland in late September. It was time to return to 'active duty'. Ron and Aggie were convinced that *Dayspring* should be sold for a larger boat and they had to give her a thorough clean. Memories of recent events faded away as they tackled the chores, unaware that God had more surprises in store for them. The 55-foot boat they had set their hearts on would soon be theirs.

7. Shipwreck

Within days of Ron and Aggie's return to Auckland, Mort Mitchell, the manager at Willow Park Christian Camp; arrived on the doorstep saying, 'A man has been looking for you two, he's been here twice already wanting to know when you were due to arrive home – he's a man with a boat.'

Aggie immediately turned to Ron and said, 'I bet you it's Jim Care. Before we left for England I told him that the Lord was going to give us his boat for our work.' A few days later the visitor returned, and Aggie triumphantly exclaimed, 'Jim Care, didn't I tell you?'

The *Innisfree* was still available but there was still much work to do on the *Dayspring*. Help was close at hand. A professional painter named Russell Knight offered his services, and a man called Luke Brough approached Ron one day when he was cleaning the topsides and said, 'I want to do all the new curtains and squabs and things'.

Ron comments, 'At the end, *Dayspring* was a real picture, she really was, so we put her up for sale, expecting to get a good price for her. We had spent weeks painting the outside and there wasn't a blemish, yet we didn't get one person to come to look at her – it was terrible.'

As Christmas drew near, however, things took a turn for the better. Jim Care agreed to take *Dayspring* in part exchange, so Ron and Aggie called a meeting with their supporters to find ways of raising the extra $11,000. Ron remembers: 'The day before the meeting a friend, Dave Harry, came knocking at the door and he was so excited as he asked, "How much do you need for the boat?" His face dropped when I told him the figure, but then he said, "Well, never mind, this is what the Lord has told me to give you." It was between $1,000 and $2,000 – I can't remember the exact figure – but when we worked it out, that left exactly $10,000 to find, so we had our meeting the next day and formed the Dayspring Trust.'

During this gathering, Ron said that he believed God wanted him to make an immediate decision on whether to buy the *Innisfree* or not. Major Thomas, founder and International Director of Capernwray Hall and the Torchbearers, stood up. He had asked to attend the meeting in an advisory capacity but he took Ron completely by surprise when he offered to provide an interest-free loan of $10,000 to complete the purchase!

That was not the end of the matter, as Ron explains. 'I remember praying specifically that God would take *Dayspring* and put her into Christian hands, and I was disappointed that we had to sell her to Jim as his heart wasn't really in her. Then, three days later, we got a telephone call from a man who said that his friend wanted to see the boat. I took the two of them out to meet Jim and this chap ended up buying *Dayspring* Three months later he became a Christian! What is more extraordinary, his three children and estranged wife also committed themselves to Christ – so we believe the Lord answered our prayer.'

For Aggie, it was the end of an era. 'We were sad to see *Dayspring* go as we had put a lot of effort into building her, and had experienced many miracles and answers to prayer during our time with her. But we

114

were very excited about *Dayspring II* and what she had to offer.' The boat had so much space and, for the first time in years, Aggie could look forward to some home comforts and privacy. She was going to travel in style from now on!

However, no sooner had Ron and Aggie bought the *Innisfree* when a survey revealed wet rot on the cabin top, and it soon became obvious that the 55-foot sloop would need a total refit. Nevertheless, friends rallied round to offer support, as Ron recalls: 'The Lord provided help and all the time there were funds coming in – it was quite incredible – we never had too much or too little, just enough.' As spring arrived the Trust continued to see God's blessing. A colleague supplied extra sails, and additional superstructure work was completed at non-commercial rates. Ron and Aggie were thankful for these provisions as they knew that the cost of running *Dayspring II* would be more than double that of *Dayspring I*.

The couple had already decided on their first port of call – Tahiti, in French Polynesia. This beautiful island of rugged mountains, waterfalls, coconut groves and coastal villages – the largest of the Society Islands – has been a French overseas territory since the mid-nineteenth century. The people are predominantly Christian but, in the late 1970s, they were almost completely untouched by Scriptures. Peter Compton, who was on leave from New Caledonia at the time, told Ron and Aggie of the tremendous spiritual needs in the area and it seemed the ideal destination for *Dayspring II*.

In his newsletter to supporters Ron wrote, 'News from Tahiti confirms that this is where God wants us to minister in the forseeable future. French and Tahitian Bibles and Christian books are in very short supply and we hope to finance a working capital of

115

$5,000 to provide a continuous stock of literature so vital to the work. The Bible Society in New Zealand will help with material on hand, but the balance will be shipped direct from France.' Scripture Gift Mission, another international Bible distributor, also provided 5,000 French and Tahitian Scripture selections valued at $224.

By April 15, *Dayspring II* had successfully completed sea trials in the Auckland Gulf and she was ready for action. At ten o'clock in the morning representatives from the Dayspring Trust, the commending Chapels, Bible Society and Capernwray assembled at Marsden Wharf for the Commissioning Service. Pastor Frank Hutchinson from Ron and Aggie's church led the congregation in prayer and the choice of hymn, 'Great is Thy Faithfulness', was particularly relevant: 'All I have needed Thy hand hath provided, Great is Thy faithfulness, Lord, unto me.' After months of working and waiting, the next chapter in the *Dayspring* ministry was about to begin.

Ron sailed out of Auckland on 29 April, arranging to meet up with Aggie in Tahiti. He remembers his crew, six Christian friends, with affection: 'We had Monty Wright, who was also a very keen yachtsman and an ideal crew member – a real tiger! If we wanted someone to go up the mast in a gale he would go. We also had Verne Wordsworth – he was seventy-five years of age and had a history of heart trouble, but his doctor told him not to miss the "trip of a lifetime". I was really glad to have Verne along as he was a wonderful man.' The others were Peter Thomas, who was taking a break from his ministry work in England, Tom Houghy, an architect from Ron's church, Kevin Palmer, a nurseryman, and Russell Knight. Everyone was eager to set sail to Tahiti although they knew it

116

would be quite a journey – some 2,250 miles north-east with different wind patterns to be faced.

During the first week *Dayspring* covered 1,000 miles with a strong south-westerly wind behind her, but the crew had been at sea only a few days when they faced their first disaster – the engine broke down. Verne Wordsworth was quick to the rescue but, on the third day, he slipped and broke some ribs and spent the next seventeen days out of action. The situation went from bad to worse when, after a period of calm, the barometer began to fall and the wind got stronger, reaching between 60 and 80 knots.

It was a very testing time. The men pulled all the sails down and, with the barometer below twenty-nine, things began to look quite desperate so Ron called everyone to prayer. It was a good idea, but then Ron started to give instructions on what to do in the 'ultimate storm' and that upset the men for a while. They drifted 180 miles backwards while laying a hull, and then they had to battle against north-easterly winds all the way to Tahiti. To make matters worse, the crew ran out of water until they were able to drain one water tank into the other. It was the strongest gale Ron had ever been in, and although *Dayspring* came through with little real damage, every one of the slides to the main sail had torn off and the men had to erect a jury rig to keep the sail up.

The voyage was one to remember, but once back on dry land the crew were able to laugh about their experiences. 'Kevin Palmer took some photographs and when we eventually got back to New Zealand he showed the slides to the local church. There was one of me, the skipper, looking absolutely filthy because I had been too busy to wash during the bad weather. Tom Houghy was standing beside me looking immaculate – shaved, with his hair combed – and when Kevin said that we had run out of water, it brought the house down!'

Ron arrived in the bustling Tahitian capital of Papeete, home to over 22,000 people of mainly Tahitian, French, and Chinese descent, just in time for the July celebrations. This was the big event of the year, when all the pastors and chiefs came in from the outlying islands for the sporting events and carnivals. Everything came to a standstill until the festivities were over, so Ron had no alternative but to make the best of things. Most of his crew had returned home but Monty and Peter remained, and Mike Hunsberger from Canada also arrived on the scene at this time. The four men got permission to run a bookstall in the middle of the city and Ron remembers, 'It was a highlight of the trip, it was absolutely incredible. Thousands of island folk flooded into the city for Bastille Day, a public holiday, and we handed them Gospels as they made their way to the canoe races, the main national sport. There was no bookshop in Papeete, even today I don't know whether there is one, and Scriptures just weren't available. All day long there was a great crowd around our table and we distributed all our Tahitian Bibles.'

Ron learned why there was such a shortage of books when he went to discuss his future programme with members of the Tahitian church, the Eglise Evangelique. They showed him a vast storehouse, absolutely crammed with books in the vernacular language, and Ron asked them, 'What do you do with all this stuff?'

They replied, 'We just wait for somebody to come along and take it away.'

Ron quickly answered, 'Well, look, would you allow the *Dayspring* to help you?'

118

The men agreed to let Ron have the material and he was able to move tens of thousands of books. One of the titles told the story of the English missionary John Williams and Ron sold twenty or thirty copies at each of the villages he later visited.

Aggie flew out to Tahiti at the end of May, and soon realised that her beautiful new boat was sadly in need of a woman's touch. 'I arrived shortly after the really rough passage and found rotten onions and apples under my bed and rotten vegetables in June-Ann's cabin – it took me ages to clean everything up!' Within days she was facing a tough schedule, for the pastors from the outlying islands wanted to know more about the *Dayspring*. 'First of all we had to present ourselves and tell them that we were there on behalf of the Bible Society of the South Pacific – to bring Bibles in the language of the people to the remote and isolated islands. We had to describe how many crew we had on board and what was our aim in reaching the villages, and what was the religion we were bringing and so on. We had quite a time of questioning, and then they decided that we should appear on the French-run television station in Papeete, so that the islands of French Polynesia could also have a good look at us, and it was quite hilarious!'

Ron and Aggie's brief moment of TV stardom gave them an unusual opportunity for witness, as Aggie recalls. 'We were seen on television by Dexter and his wife Bridget, a young couple who had been excommunicated from the Mormon Church. They had since accepted the Lord Jesus Christ as their personal Saviour but, although they had a Bible, they were waiting for someone to bring them real fellowship in the Word of God. They were so excited to see us and they came round to the boat the very next day – they were so hungry for God's Word. We had Bible studies every night and we were really blessed by their enthusiasm in such a far outreach.'

The on-going ministry among yachties also continued and Ron and Aggie met people of all nationalities – Germans, Americans, Japanese, French, Marquesans and Dutch. The couple usually broke bread every Sunday with a French Tahitian family, who came aboard to have fellowship and to share in God's Word with the people from the yachts. There was a wide ministry and June-Ann also enjoyed the company as she was able to mix with the children moored nearby.

Aggie was also pleased to receive some unexpected help with her daughter's education. June-Ann had never been to school and, although she studied regularly by means of a correspondence course, Aggie often had to find time to teach her herself. She comments, 'It was very difficult but we thank the Lord Jesus for sending the right teachers along. We had Peter Thomas as an English and Maths teacher, so I was relieved of teaching her those subjects, which is always wonderful!'

Peter was a great help in another way. Ron hoped to take a local pastor on his tour of the French Polynesian islands but the Eglise Evangelique could not find anyone to go. In the end, Ron had to rely heavily on Peter as he was the only one who spoke French!

The *Dayspring* finally left Papeete in August, by which time Ron had begun to realise the enormity of the task before him. Eastern Polynesia is made up of five archipelagos – the Society Islands, which include Tahiti, the Tuamotus, the Marquesas, the Gambier Islands, and the Australs – all scattered over an immense area of the south-eastern Pacific. In a newsletter to friends Ron wrote, 'The vastness of this region did not really come through to us until we began a detailed study. The needs of this area are enormous and we are so small. The challenges facing us in 1979 seem almost impossible to achieve. We know it is only your support and the power of Christ that will make these plans attainable.'

The Russells received a warm welcome in the first port of call, the seventy-nine coral islands of the Northern Tuamotos where, thanks to the Bible Society films and Peter's French, they were able to communicate with the atoll dwellers. When Ron sailed on to the mountainous islands of the Marquesas, however, he almost came up against a solid wall. 'The Roman Catholic bishop received us kindly and gave us a letter of introduction to the village chiefs, but he told us that we had no hope of selling any Tahitian material, although we might be able to sell some French. We managed to persuade him that we ought to distribute our Scriptures and it turned out that he was absolutely wrong – the people wanted the books, I think because they listened to Tahitian on the radio.'

In addition to the obvious Spiritual needs, the environment was notoriously hostile. Ron wrote to Tony Hanne in Auckland, telling him, 'Each set of islands has its special circumstances. The landing on most of the beaches is impossible owing to the tremendous surf.' Peter had returned to England, and Ron and Aggie had to rely heavily on Mike Hunsberger, as Aggie remembers: 'We thank God for Mike's courage and perseverance. As well as having to put up with our small family, he had some hard anchorages in the Marquesas Islands, We used to have to glare into the beaches to see where there was a clearing as the surf was always rolling, so it was a dreadful place to land – there was never any calm. These were really trying times for Mike – the anchorages were hard, the language was hard, and Ron had to stay with the ship because it was rolling so much.'

The small team had a particularly hair-raising experience in one of the islands, where they were due to attend a meeting in a large Catholic church. They rowed ashore in the early evening but the landing was not smooth, as Aggie recalls. 'We knew that when we got to the beach we would have to really move because, if we didn't, the surf would just take us and the dinghy off, but even we weren't prepared for what happened! It was about half-past six and we were due at the meeting at half-past seven, but we didn't arrive until about eight-thirty, because we were tumbled over in the surfs about three times. One time it was really touch and go – we nearly lost Ron and I didn't know whether June-Ann was alive or not until I saw her on the beach!'

As soon as Aggie reached dry land she looked around for Ron. He was nowhere to be seen so she called to Mike, 'Quick, I think he's under the dinghy.' Sure enough, when they lifted it up there he was, jammed in by the rolling surfs. Ron was safe but the torch, the paddle, and all the shoes had been lost. Luckily Ron and Mike had delivered the equipment during daylight, otherwise the damage might have been more severe. When the *Dayspring* team finally arrived at the church they were soaking wet but there was nowhere to dry off, so they remained in their bedraggled state for some three hours!

The return journey was no better. 'When it was time to come home at nearly midnight,' Aggie remembers, 'we couldn't get back! We tumbled over three or four times, we just couldn't go against the surf, and we didn't know how to reach the boat. I told Ron, "If I get back to the boat alive, I'm not coming back to these shores!" It was so dangerous! But then

Mike found a small pier and he said, "I think we'd better try it." So we went to this little stone pier and, as the surfs rose, one jumped in and then another and it took us three attempts to get back to the boat. We almost lost our lives, but God has been really wonderful, helping us through such danger.'

On land, however, Aggie excelled, as Ron remembers: 'She found it a little trying not being able to get ashore. Haniapa Bay was an exception and she spent the whole day talking to the ladies under the palm trees. It was just wonderful to see her preaching with just a few French words, a few Marquesan, and a great deal of gestures.'

By Christmas 1978 the *Dayspring* team were back in Tahiti because of an unusual 'postal strike'. Ron had been waiting for a chart to get to other islands but he had received no letters or Bibles for three months. He kept ringing John Doom, the Bible Society representative, who insisted that everything was being sent regularly. When the Russells finally arrived at John's office, he told them that he had taken things to the airport every week. Ron decided to investigate and made his way to the airfield where, in the corner of one of the hangars, he found an enormous pile of Scriptures, letters, and other packages for *Dayspring*. Apparently, every time the supply plane flew out to the Marquesas it was full, so the Russell's material had been left behind!

January was spent refitting *Dayspring* and visiting local churches, but by February Ron and Aggie were on their travels once again, to Raiatea, the second largest of the Society Islands. Ron has fond memories of the minister there. 'Once ashore, we piled all our Scriptures into his house and settled down for something to eat. As we sat having our meal, he turned round and said to me, "Oh, by the way, you are a real captain, aren't you?" So I had to reluctantly tell him that I wasn't, just an ordinary yachtsman. He seemed quite happy with that, but after a while he leaned across the table and said, "But you are a real minister?" And again I had to apologise and say, "No, I'm just a layman." Anyway, off we went to the church, and during his introduction, the minister stood up and said, "Now, I would like to introduce you to the Rev. Captain Ron Russell!" That's the sort of thing we are up against in the islands – the protocol is very important and the people can't lose face, so I suddenly acquired a peak cap and a dog collar!'

From Raiatea, the *Dayspring* team set off for the Austral Islands, a tiny volcanic group about 300 miles south of Tahiti. They were joined by an American called Dave Harding and everyone was in high spirits. Ron had managed to get hold of 500 Tahitian Bibles flown out especially from Hong Kong. At last they had some 'ammunition', some real Tahitian Bibles to take to the islanders. However, as soon as Ron rounded the corner of Tahiti the wind changed, and Aggie realised she was in for a very rough trip indeed.

'The wind became really strong,' Ron remembers, 'and we were laid right over. Aggie was quite seasick and frightened and she pleaded with me to go back, but I wouldn't because it was such a good wind. She disappeared down below and the wind really blew – I remember seeing her hanging on to the pillar, with all her knuckles showing and she was petrified.'

Aggie continues: 'I said to Ron, "Please turn back, I've had enough," but he wouldn't, so I went down below and asked God to give me strength. I also asked His forgiveness for doubting – for all those years he had carried us through storms and hurricanes and yet, one little hiccup of four days, and I wanted to give up. Then I found the verse in the Scriptures that talks about the storms and the peace within and for the first time it really meant something to me. We sailed on and after a couple of days I got up. By this time we were inside the passage, and the first thing I saw was a beautiful lagoon!'

The *Dayspring* had arrived at Raivavae, the 'beauty spot' of the Australs. As Ron and Aggie sailed into the lagoon they noticed a huge crowd – over a thousand people – waiting patiently on the concrete wharf. Exhausted from their journey the Russells sailed on to find a quiet anchorage but, as the hours passed, Aggie suddenly realised that the people were still there. When she and Ron finally went ashore they were horrified to find that the islanders had been waiting for the *Dayspring*. Ron adds, 'The whole island had turned out in their Sunday best and had been waiting while we took it easy – it wasn't a very good start. It just goes to show how keen they are. The Austral islanders are very isolated and they are really eager to see people. We left nine days later greatly encouraged and deeply thankful to God.'

The enthusiasm continued in the islands of Tubuai and Rurutu but it was the last island in the Australs, Rimatara, that was to have a special place in Ron's heart. 'There was something unique about Rimatara – 600 of the loveliest Christians live there, surrounded by a steep reef where the surf roars day and night. We had been told by the Eglise Evangelique that the pastor was really old so we didn't know what to expect, but he was a very godly man and I had never met so many dedicated Christians on one small island.'

On arrival, Ron had to anchor precariously off the reef and wait for the islanders to come out to the boat. He waited six hours, separated from the shore by one incredible wall of surf, before he finally made contact.

He remembers, 'How anyone can come out of that I don't know. At about four o'clock in the afternoon we saw a huge twelve-man canoe shoot across the surf – the islanders can only come across twice a day, when the tide is just right. They took us ashore and, once we were safely on land, they lit a fire in front of us and put leaves on top to make a smokescreen – we had to walk through it to be cleansed by the smoke.'

At first, the islanders' response to the *Dayspring* cargo was puzzling. As this was Ron's last port of call in French Polynesia, he had taken everything ashore, spreading the Scriptures out on large tables in one of the huts. He was perplexed when the islanders just walked round and round for about twenty minutes, looking and talking amongst themselves. In the end Ron said, 'Well, what's wrong?'

They replied, 'There's just one problem – there's not enough! This is enough for this village, but there are two others.' With that, the islanders sat for the next hour making three identical heaps for each village, right down to the last portion!

When the Russells left four days later they had sold everything on board. They were thrilled with the response but, once again, they had to brave the surf. 'It was quite spectacular. They only time we could leave was midnight when the waves were going down. The islanders got four jeeps and they all came to the beach together to shine their lights onto the roaring surf – it must have been quite a sight. We had to wait until the right time before we could make our move and one old man there, the "master of the surf", agreed to tell us when it was safe to be on our way. The moment he said "Go", off we went as fast as we could!'

The next port of call, the Cook Islands, had an even tougher terrain. The sixteen coral islands cover an area of 1,000 miles, but Penrhyn is the only one to offer safe anchorage. *Dayspring* had to drift or cling precariously to the coral ledge throughout the whole six-week trip. Ron had already agreed that Aggie should take June-Ann back to Suva, and it was just as well. In a newsletter written on 30 June 1979, he wrote, 'Greetings from gale-swept Rarotonga. At the moment the barometer continues to fall after five hectic days in Avatiu Harbour – a hole in the reef jammed packed full of vessels and the only safe haven in the whole of the Cook Island Group. Every couple of months or so the wind shifts from south-easterly round to north-westerly and it really blows! One night we were in a 50-knot north-wester and the waves were crashing in on us. We were anchored in front of ten other yachts and, if our anchor had drifted, we would have crashed into them all! It was quite an adventure getting out of there, but the engine came into its own and took us into the open sea.'

It was no wonder that the *Dayspring* crew had such a rough time in Rarotonga as the rainclouds hang over this highly fertile volcanic island for much of the year. Despite the weather the Maori islanders, closely related to the New Zealand Maoris, are a friendly race and Ron received a warm welcome from the Bible Society representative, Father Damien. But he did meet one awkward customer, a chap in control of the Bibles who was very reluctant to give copies away. Even when Ron finally managed to get 300 Maori and 200 English Bibles, he had to ration them because the demand was so great. There were no anchorages so Dave and Mike took turns to go ashore, and time after time they would come back to Ron pleading for more Bibles, but there were just none to spare.

Ron managed to visit every island in the Cooks, but sometimes the welcome in the outlying atolls was rather too enthusiastic. At one island, every time the

Dayspring drifted close to shore, canoes full of boys would come out and the crew would have to entertain them in the cockpit. One evening it was getting late and the men were feeling a bit weary so, when they saw another group coming, they decided to go offshore. About an hour later they could see no one on the beach so they drifted back again, but soon the islanders spotted them and came paddling out.

Ron slipped below to get some sleep but then began to feel guilty, so he went up and started talking to the young lads. They said something that really rocked Ron, as he remembers: 'I asked why people just sat on the wharf staring out at the boat for hours, and these kids replied, "Don't you realise that we are so lonely?" I said, "But you've got each other, haven't you?" and they said, "Yes, but we don't see anyone from the outside world, sometimes for six months!"

'Suddenly, I realised that they were pleased to see any visitors, regardless of what they did. That really jolted me and I realised how selfish I had been – but you do get tired.'

July 1979 was a month of farewells. Mike travelled to New Zealand to spend some time at the Capernwray centre and Dave went home to the United States. Ron sailed back to Fiji to sit out the hurricane season, but, once at Suva, he received a pleasant surprise. Aggie had received a letter from Larry Reed, the American 'philosopher' the Russells had first met five years earlier, and he had become a Christian.

Ron takes up the story, 'Apparently, some time after we left him Larry had a quarrel with his wife and decided to sail back to America single-handed. He got into some really bad weather on the way to Hawaii and the boat began to leak badly. He was at his wits' end when he noticed the Bible we had given him.

128

Larry took it off the shelf and began to read it. He re-dedicated his life to Christ right there, in the middle of the ocean, and his letter said that he had since been to Bible school and was now an active Christian. That was a wonderful homecoming for me. If you place the Bible into people's hands believing that God can use it, it really can happen.'

Shortly after receiving Larry's letter, Ron busied himself with plans for the future. He would tour the Fijian islands from October to February, haul out and refit in March, and then visit Tonga and the New Hebrides during the remainder of 1980. Aggie, June-Ann, and three young evangelists joined Ron for his trip around Fiji and they eventually met up with their old friend, Maika Bovoro. 'The response in each village was quite tremendous,' Ron recalls. 'Maika, tireless as always in his zeal for the Lord, continued daily into the early hours to teach young and old alike. He spoke of the Bible Society's work and, most important of all, told his audience that the Word of God comes alive when it is used. The trip was very successful and we managed to sell 500 Bibles and New Testaments as well as a great deal of books and Bible helps.'

During the trip, however, the *Dayspring* team were never far from danger. Whilst on a tour of the island of Koro, Ron tailed into a reef at dawn, embayed by winds of 50 knots, and had to fight clear under storm canvas. 'We gave God all the glory as we saw a group of village folk, headed by Maika, praying on the shore for our safety.'

Prayer also came to the rescue a few days later. Aggie, who had been ashore with the evangelists for the day, returned to the beach at midnight, only to find that the dinghy had been swept away. The whole village turned out to help, and following a prayer meeting some of the islanders formed a search party. When their efforts proved fruitless they decided to turn for home. Then nature gave a helping hand. Aggie remembers, 'It was an overcast night but then the moon poked out from between the clouds and the whole sea lit up. The dinghy, which was made of aluminium, caught the light and, suddenly, there she was!'

On arrival back at Suva, the *Dayspring* had a rendezvous with the *Logos*, the ship owned by the international Christian group, Operation Mobilisation. 'We complement each other,' Ron explains, 'because we are both boat ministries, but *Logos* sails to the coastal cities and we visit the remote islands. We planned to take a ten-day trip around the villages of Mbengga, home of the Fijian firewalkers, with some of the *Logos* crew, but on the way everything went wrong! The cylinder head gasket blew and the mainsail ripped in half, so I had to stay behind to do the repairs with Rob Clark, the second engineer from the *Logos*, while Aggie and the crew went ashore.'

It was a difficult time. The small 'land team' got into the dinghy and waded into the swamps to get to the first village, where they stayed for two days and nights. Aggie held her Bible stall and meeting but, when she came back the *Dayspring* was still not repaired. There was no engine power and the yacht had to go in among the reefs. Everyone was very tense but there were no mishaps. In fact, during the trip Aggie had a very good meeting with the churches and also met a firewalker – one of the very big chiefs who had come to know Christ.

The whole episode was an experience for the *Logos* boys, she recalls, 'because, in their ministry everything is loaded in trucks and they just drive their Scriptures to the destination. With the *Dayspring*, everything is man-handled and we have to walk several miles with our equipment and lift the dinghy over reefs and such like. The *Logos* team thought it was pretty hard work and I was glad that someone finally had a bit of sympathy for us!'

The trip was a short one because the *Dayspring* was in urgent need of repair, so the Russells returned to Suva. Aggie continues: 'Rob Clark stayed with us and other engineers came from the *Logos* to mend our engine. It was wonderful how the Lord supplied the right people to do the job. Parts had to be ordered and they came just at the last minute – everything was beautifully timed. Rob just had time to fit the engine before the *Logos* left port for pastures new! The *Logos* crew presented Ron with a sextant – one of the best of its kind in the world – and he was really thrilled. We had good fellowship with *Logos* and we are still in touch with them.'

Despite the mishaps, things went well during the early part of 1980 and, right on schedule, Ron set sail for the island kingdom of Tonga on 11 May. He was accompanied by his old friend Mike Hunsberger, who had come back from Capernwray especially for the trip, and Brian Snider. Aggie planned to fly out to meet them a week later. *Dayspring* was in tip-top condition. Her engine had been completely overhauled and she had new sails from Hong Kong. She was also well stocked with food, 700 Tongan Bibles and a variety of Christian books. Ron was looking forward to an exciting trip but his boat never reached her destination. On 15 May, amid bad weather and poor visibility, she hit the Vuata reef seven miles west-south-west of the remote Fijian island of Ono-i-Lau.

It was early evening when Brian took the wheel while Ron and Mike went below to rest. The wind was strong and huge waves pounded the *Dayspring* as she travelled southward. Suddenly there was a crash and Ron awoke to find himself in total darkness, wedged between the galley and the freezer. He remembers, 'It was a shattering experience – just like being in an earthquake. The whole boat was turning around and the waves were coming right over us.' *Dayspring* was on her side and the life-raft and dinghy had been swept away on impact, so the three men huddled together in oily water, wondering what to do next.

'There we were,' Ron recalls, 'completely marooned and at the mercy of God. We sat on the edge of the boat – she looked as if she might break up at any minute. We were shivering with cold and fright so we pulled a sail right over us. Mike called us to prayer and we really thought the end had come. I said, "Well, Lord, this is Your boat. And if it is Your plan that we should come to You now, well, let Your will be done." The waves were crashing right over us and we had to tie ourselves on, and yet it was a marvellous experience in some ways. Half of me was sad because I was not going to see my wife and daughter any more, but the other half was looking forward to being with the Lord!'

After the prayer meeting Ron pulled back the sail. Suddenly he realised that the lights were on. If the batteries were still working he could use the radio. He remembers, 'I radioed back to Suva: "Mayday, Mayday." They were notorious for not answering, but this time they answered immediately. We said that the boat was on the reef and might not last another high tide. They woke up the Bible Society, who woke up Aggie, and Aggie woke up the rest of Suva! We had everyone our side.'

Then the three men waited for what seemed an eternity. At four o'clock in the morning they saw a plane in the distance and sent up two flares – the only dry ones on board. The plane didn't see them, and as Ron tried to radio again, he could see that the water was beginning to reach the batteries. Soon there would be no way of communicating with the outside world. Were they to be left stranded in one of the remotest areas of Fiji after all?

Help was close by, however. Unknown to Ron a Fijian medical vessel, the *Nasi Yalodina* (*Loyal Nurse*), had been sheltering nearby. Within a matter of hours she had arrived on the scene and, negotiating the reef, her crew managed to get Ron, Mike and Brian safely on board. Within no time they were back at Ono-i-Lau. It was a wonderful coincidence that the first plane ever to touch down on the island's newly-built airstrip was arriving the very next morning. After he had delivered his cargo, some lighting equipment for the airstrip, the pilot took Ron and his colleagues back to Suva. Within twelve hours they were back in Fiji – bruised and battered, but otherwise unhurt.

The rescue had been spectacular, but once back on dry land Ron faced the bleak facts. *Dayspring* had been more than a boat – it was the only home that he and Aggie had. Now she was lying smashed on a reef and all the family possessions were with her. To make matters worse, all the other yachties were laughing and saying, 'Where is your God?' For the first time in years Ron began to doubt the future. He just could not understand why the Lord had taken his boat away.

Mike

8. *Dayspring III*

'I have been in three shipwrecks, and once I spent twenty-four hours in the water. In my many travels, I have been in danger from floods and from robbers, in danger from fellow-Jews and from Gentiles; there have been dangers in the cities, dangers in the wilds, dangers on the high seas, and dangers from false friends' (2 Cor. 11.25–26 GNB).

Ron came across this passage in the Bible shortly after his return to Auckland. He was feeling sorry for himself until this reminder of Paul's suffering made him realise that God had no time for self-pity. *Dayspring* was gone, but the ministry had to continue. A few days later Ron joined Eric and Grace Dowdall aboard their 40-foot motor yacht *Staretta* for a return trip to the site of the shipwreck. *Dayspring*'s starboard side was lying partly out of the water, and the small 'rescue team' found a large supply of unspoilt Scriptures. Crossing the reef again and again in breaking surf, they managed to salvage 600 Bibles and $1,200 worth of Christian books, as well as the generator and some charts. Things were looking up again, and within a matter of months Ron and Aggie had seen a fitting replacement for *Dayspring II*.

Sundowner, a 74-foot steel ketch built in 1969 and used extensively among the Indonesian islands, was full of rust. Nevertheless it was large, with plenty of accommodation space, and Ron was impressed by the individual engine room and workshop. By this time he and Aggie felt led to a larger vessel because they hoped to develop an outreach programme during the summer months. First, however, they had to get the church elders to come and have a look and, frankly, the elders were not impressed. One said 'What do you want with this big hunk of a boat? Surely we could look for something else.' There was so much work to be done, but once again Aggie was convinced that God wanted the *Sundowner* for the Pacific.

The boat was not cheap – it was initially priced at $110,000. Once again, the Russells received 'miraculous' financial aid. Unknown to Ron, an anonymous English Christian had paid the insurance fees on *Dayspring II* shortly before the shipwreck. The boat was actually insured for $90,000! The money came through at the end of October. The United Bible Societies (UBS) also provided a substantial interest-free loan, so Ron and Aggie were able to purchase the *Sundowner* for $87,000 in the December of 1980. There was an added bonus. The UBS loan meant that they could use their own money, which they had loaned to the Dayspring Trust, to buy something they needed more than ever – a home of their own!

'God provided a house in such an incredible way,' Ron remembers, 'in a district which was very near the school we wanted June-Ann to go to – Macleans College, one of the best in Auckland and with a Christian headmaster.' This was a great benefit to June-Ann because she had been doing correspondence courses for years and now, at thirteen, she needed a traditional education. A boat ministry was not the ideal environment for a child, and Aggie recalls some of the frustrations her daughter suffered during those long years at sea. 'I remember the correspondence teacher asking me to get June-Ann to write down all her thoughts – she wanted to see what the girl was really thinking. June-Ann was on her own a lot and didn't really have anyone to share her feelings with. One day I saw a note in her handwriting which said, "All we see is sea, sea, sea, and I'm sick of it!" This really made me laugh, but she had to tell somebody as she couldn't tell Ron and me.'

As Aggie had no great love of the sea herself she was, like June-Ann, really grateful for a land-based home. 'I kept pinching myself when I saw the house. I had never dreamed of having a home since coming to know Jesus Christ, as I believed that my life was in the mission field with the boat. The house was a real gift from Him - free of mortgage with no strings attached! It's wonderful to be able to come home and put our feet on firm ground for a little while from time to time and say, "This is our own little nest which Christ has provided." Nothing posh, but very comfortable and very cosy.'

With the purchase of the house, the time had come to agree a new strategy. The Russells decided that, for the next five years, they would help the Bible Society on a six-monthly basis. Ron would sail out to the islands in April, returning to New Zealand each November to avoid the hurricane season. During the summer months he could concentrate on refitting the boat, and developing a sailing school programme. Aggie would use the local air services to fly out to the *Dayspring* at regular intervals. This would allow her to spend longer periods with June-Ann and with Peter, her son from her first marriage whom she and Ron had adopted when he was sixteen years of age.

After a traumatic year the future was beginning to take shape, but first of all, Ron and Aggie had to seek out some volunteers to help them knock the

Sundowner into shape. It was at this time that Allan Pfeiffer, a young South Australian farmer who had been doing missionary work in the Fijian islands, appeared on the scene. He remembers his first encounter with *Dayspring III*. 'I first saw the boat about a week after Ron and Aggie had met with the elders. They had to have a survey to check the hull out before they signed the final purchasing papers. I had my doubts and fears when they first approached me as I had never done anything on boats before and this was all new. When I first saw it I thought, "It's so big, I can't handle this." But, like Ron and Aggie and many others who trust the Lord, I knew He was telling me, "I know you can't handle it, but I can!" '

Allan soon became enthusiastic about the project, although there were very real problems, as he explains. 'The boat was a real mess – no electricity, only kerosene lanterns, and one or two lights that you hooked up with clips onto batteries. The toilet was operational but you needed a licence to use it! There was no real running water, we had to pump everything out of barrels. In general, every porthole and hatch leaked! There was no ventilation and we wondered how the previous owners had ever survived in the tropics.'

There was much to be done but, once again, God provided the manpower to continue the work. Len Brys, one of the partners of the Voss and Brys shipyard who had helped the Russells with *Dayspring II*, was very helpful and there were others. Verne Wordsworth was seventy-eight years old but he used to arrive every day at ten a.m. and work through until five o'clock – he was a wonderful example to everyone. John Vlaanderen, a retired businessman from Auckland, and Kevin Muller, a young Australian who was previously bosun of the *Logos*, also helped out. Jack

139

Roberts, Ron's old friend from the early days, took on the role of ship's cook, and Kevin Palmer, a nursery manager from Auckland, did much of the final finishing work.

Despite the help, however, tempers did sometimes wear thin, as Aggie remembers. 'Ron used to come home and tell me off for choosing a boat which needed so much done to it. He used to say, "You chose this boat and it's so expensive, everything we need to buy is double the price!" I never doubted that it was the Lord's boat so I didn't worry, but then I didn't have to do the hard work – I left that to the men and just prayed! Once I remember going down to the boat and finding Allan absolutely black from top to bottom. But, in spite of everything, the Lord didn't let us down. He always provided, even though Ron kept moaning to me, "This is your choice!"'

Right up to the last moment there were technical hitches, and a strike delayed the delivery of Ron and Aggie's one claim to luxury – a deep freeze unit. Another problem was rust. The Russells had little experience of steel boats and they made the mistake of only inspecting the inside of the *Sundowner*. Ron comments, 'In retrospect, I think we could have paid a lot less for it and used that money to do other things. But years later, it is still OK. We've had our moments of doubt, but the Lord has always provided and we've never really been in financial trouble with repairs.'

The yacht was finally commissioned on 17 May 1981, just a year after the shipwreck of *Dayspring II*. The gathering at the inaugural ceremony in the Voss and Brys shipyard included Christian friends and Mr Colin Reed, General Secretary of the Bible Society of New Zealand. In his address, Colin Reed likened the attitude of the *Dayspring* crew to Moses who, thousands of years earlier, had said to God, 'If you do not go with us, don't make us leave this place.' But the Lord had replied, 'I will go with you, and I will give you victory' (Exod. 33.14, 15 GNB).

It had been a decade since Ron and Aggie had first embarked on their seafaring ministry. Two boats had come and gone and there had been other changes. Just five months earlier Maika Bovoro had resigned as Executive Secretary of the Bible Society. His successor was Inoke Kubuabola, a former rugby player who had become a Christian while attending university in New Zealand. Maika went to join World Vision and Ron and Aggie knew they had lost a valued friend. As they prepared to launch the third *Dayspring* vessel, however, the couple were confident that God was indeed still with them and that there was much to do in the Pacific.

As the captain of a much bigger vessel, Ron needed a larger crew than ever before, and for the first time, he faced unexpected pressures at sea. During the maiden voyage there were nine men aboard and, although they included Ron's old friends Mase Teoneo and Jack Roberts, some were quick to criticise his way of doing things. Allan comments, 'It always causes friction when the men disagree with the skipper and the problem tends to be magnified because everyone is living in such close quarters. These tensions do bring out people's characters, and I remember that those who were close to the Lord really stood out during that voyage.'

When Aggie joined Ron at Tuvalu, the first port of call, she was faced with a new set of problems. She had to check the crew's behaviour on land because they did not always dress or behave as they should. The *Dayspring* team had to spend some four or five days ashore and the anchorages were hard – often the boat was just hanging off the sheer shelf of a coral reef ledge. It was a nerve-racking situation, and one that required constant vigilance from whoever was on 'anchor watch'. Needless to say, there were many anxious moments and frustrations.

Despite the tensions, Ron remembers one crew member with particular affection. 'Mort Mitchell had been the manager of the local Christian camp in Auckland before retiring and he was wonderful, a great cook. The only trouble was that he suffered with asthma, and once or twice at night, he was really bad. It used to worry me, but he said that he had been like that all his life, so I just had to get used to it. The one thing he had never mastered at camp was public speaking. He got thrown right into it in Tuvalu and he really came out on top!'

The Tuvaluan welcome was as enthusiastic as ever. Since Ron's last visit in 1974 the mainly Polynesian people had witnessed two outstanding events: political independence from Britain and the translation of the New Testament into their mother tongue. They were happy to spend a few days welcoming their visitors, and as soon as the crew arrived on dry land, the Church opened the door wide to receive God's Word and ministry. Each island participated in a full programme of Bible study for all age groups, and in moving speeches many islanders confessed to a new awakening through Jesus Christ.

The Bible table was available as always and the *Dayspring* team sold 476 Bibles and 377 New Testaments, as well as distributing 2,500 gospels of Luke. They also made effective use of a new Bible Society resource, 'Jesus', a 16mm film produced by Campus Crusade for Christ. It was dubbed in six Pacific island languages and proved to be a wonderful springboard for discussions with the islanders.

Ron was pleased to be able to reach Nukulaelae, the last island in the group, which he had missed completely during his first voyage in *Dayspring I*. He remembers, 'When we finally arrived they were determined to put on a show of hospitality – dancing and singing – and they treated us like royalty. We had a wonderful four or five days with them and that' s where I met the little girl Dayspring. They have a habit in the islands of commemorating events in the naming of the children, and as one girl was born at the time of our intended visit they named her after the boat!'

The Russells had a nasty shock when they finally made their way back to the beach at the end of their stay. The chief's son had taken their dinghy to go and look at the boat and, as Ron and Aggie arrived on the scene, he was paddling towards the very spot where the islanders were trying to dynamite a passage through the reef. The couple watched helplessly as a sudden explosion disturbed the wave pattern. The dinghy capsized, throwing the chief's son and all the *Dayspring* equipment into the water. Thankfully, no one was hurt, and Ron was able to salvage the projector, generator, and some of the films. The Samoan version of 'Jesus' and many of the Bibles had been ruined, but such was their enthusiasm for the Word of God that the islanders rushed to the beach to claim the soggy books. It was ironic that Allan's camera was in the kit that got blown, and the only photo that survived the soaking was of Ron with the little girl, Dayspring!

The Tuvaluan tour ended, literally, with a bang, and as he was unable to obtain extra supplies of Scriptures, Ron decided to head back to Suva while Aggie flew on to New Zealand. Once back in Fiji, he met up with the Rev. Inoke Nabulivou, President of the Fijian Methodist Church, and they set off for a tour of the Lau Islands. Here the *Dayspring* crew managed to distribute 150 Bibles and 300 New Testaments before returning home to New Zealand in November. Despite the trials and tribulations, the first year aboard the new boat had gone well after all.

One thing that impressed Allan on the trip was the opportunity to witness to yachties. 'One day when we were anchored in Suva this chap, I can't remember if he was American or Australian, came across and asked if we were Bible folk. My immediate thought was that he was going to mock us but then he said, "I want to trade two books for a Bible – I've read portions of Scripture but I've never read the whole Bible." It turned out that he had been diving off an oil rig and had seen a Scripture portion on the sea bed. It was open at the point: "Render therefore unto Caesar the things which are Caesar's and unto God the things that are God's" (Matt. 22.21 AV). The Word of God is really powerful because that one portion led the man to seek out more about the Bible! We also gave a portion to a young European girl who was really into cults – only time will tell if she will change, it's not our job to reap the harvest, only to sow the seed.'

1982 opened on a sad note for Ron and Aggie. Mort Mitchell, who had returned to his wife and children in December, died. Ron remembers, 'Mort had an asthma attack which caused a heart attack and he was taken from us – it was a terrible blow. However, he had spent part of the last year of his life aboard the *Dayspring* and I think he really enjoyed it.'

By February the Russells were hard at work again. *Dayspring III* was moored in the Tamaki River and needed a lot of attention. Ron had to overhaul the rigging, masts and deck gear to comply with New Zealand's strict sailing regulations. He was back in

Fiji two months later, making plans to visit Kiribati for a three-month distribution programme. Allan Pfeiffer and Rob Fischer acted as permanent crew, and Kevin Palmer and some Bible students from Canada helped out at various stages during the voyage.

Once again, Aggie joined the *Dayspring* for a brief visit to the Fijian island of Rotuma, where she and Ron found yet another namesake. During their first visit some five years earlier, the islanders had been very upset because they were unable to transport the Russells to the villages. In the intervening years they had acquired a small pick-up which they promptly named Dayspring! The truck had gone over a cliff just before Ron and Aggie arrived but it was still in working order, and the couple were able to visit the whole area with Scriptures. At one stage, however, the engine overheated and Dayspring came to a standstill. Amazingly, it chose the very spot where some ladies were holding a Bible meeting. They made the most of this 'heaven-sent' opportunity and bought masses of Bibles!

When Aggie returned to New Zealand, she gave a full report of the Tuvaluan trip to the local Bible Society. 'Ron had a distribution workshop where he spoke to about sixty members of a Methodist youth group. The next morning, twenty turned up and did Scripture distribution in the hospitals and towns. It was good to hear their testimony, and they confessed that it was the first time they had witnessed openly for Christ. We were thrilled and thanked the Lord Jesus for this tremendous opportunity.'

Ron sailed on to Micronesia with an extra passenger on board, Shadrack Bera, a tireless Christian worker from Fiji who acted as both evangelist and crew. The voyage was pleasant enough, but on arrival at Kiribati Ron ended up being questioned in jail while his crew waited for him under a coconut tree! 'It all happened because, when I went ashore to clear customs, the immigration people told me that I didn't need to see the local doctor. However, there was some sort of rivalry going on because, as soon as the crew actually set foot on shore, we found the doctor waiting there with a police constable. They thought I hadn't gone through the proper channels, and they arrested me! I had to make a long statement and then the rumour went around the islands that I tried to bring a dog ashore.'

Despite this encounter with the authorities, Ron received a lot of help from the Kiribati Protestant Church, and each of the remote islands in the group gave the crew a warm welcome. Pastors, elders and other church leaders travelled miles to gather at the main village, where the *Dayspring* team held their three-day programme of Scripture distribution, Bible studies and events for younger people. Ron continues, 'The more we go to these islands the more friendly the people become. They are very deep-thinking and hard to get to know, but when they talk about spiritual things they seem to have a much deeper conviction.'

The *Dayspring* team had an unnerving experience one day when they began to talk about the second coming of Christ to the islanders of Tabiteuea. The pastors rushed them away, and Ron later learned that a hundred years before there had almost been a civil war in the area because someone had predicted Christ's return and nothing had happened. Now the people were not even allowed to mention the subject, even though it was in the Bible!

Things were better at the northernmost island of Makin. 'We had a wonderful time there. On the first day the islanders held their celebrations, but when we said that we wanted to teach spiritual things, they

146

soon got down to work. There was an avenue of trees from the meeting house down to the sandy beach – you could look back and see the boat just hanging off the reef, a great setting.'

It was also dangerous. After three days the wind swung north-west and Ron had to make a hasty retreat back to *Dayspring* to stop it from crashing onto the reef. From that time the weather took a turn for the worse and, realising that he would be unable to reach the four remote islands in the south, Ron decided to head back to Fiji.

As 1982 drew to a close Ron was able to report to the Bible Society, 'We have sold and distributed nearly all the Scripture portions we had on the yacht. At the last island, we sold 90 pocket New Testaments to the Seventh Day Adventist school, and some 200 school children aged between 13 and 17 came to hear us talk,'

The following spring was an eventful one for the Bible Society in the South Pacific. In March, Cyclone Oscar hit the Fiji Islands, leaving a trail of destruction in its wake. Some 200,000 people had to live on emergency rations, and schools and tourist hotels were converted into relief centres. The UBS quickly launched an emergency appeal, enabling the Bible Society to distribute free Bibles to every home affected by the disaster.

Ron was not involved in this operation, as he had already made plans to undertake a major tour of New Caledonia and the Solomons with Allan Pfeiffer and Jeff Roberts. The trip was to mark a watershed in *Dayspring*'s history. Until now, Ron had always enjoyed easy access to the Pacific, but times were changing. Because of the rising tide of nationalism, many island authorities would no longer be keen to welcome outsiders. Even when Ron did gain access, he was to find that some islanders were more interested in politics than the Bible.

The problem flrst became apparent in New Caledonia, where trouble had been brewing because the Melanesian sector of the population wanted independence from France. As soon as Ron arrived in the capital of Noumea, his old friend Peter Compton, the Bible Society committee and local church leaders worked hard to make his stay as profitable as possible. Aggie and June-Ann flew out to meet the crew and the small party set up a Scripture stall on the wharf in full view of their 'Bible Boat'. Everything went well and they met with a great deal of success but, time and again the people asked for their views on the political situation.

The same thing happened when Ron sailed north towards Vanuatu, stopping at the Loyalty Islands on the way. At Lifou a day of Bible study, prayer and fellowship attracted forty young people but the meeting was marred by an islander who wanted to discuss the independence issue. The reception at the next port of call, Ouvea, was better and the crew were able to sell Scriptures outside a Roman Catholic mission. One sister purchased fifteen Bibles for a remote village on the other side of the lagoon and Ron managed to distribute all his stock before returning to the boat.

Ron wondered if politics would rear its head again in Vanuatu. After years of British and French rule, the island group had become a republic in 1980, but the democratically elected Vanuaaka party faced strong opposition from separatist groups. Although an uprising led by flamboyant rebel leader Jimmy Stevens had been quashed, the raising of the new flag on Independence Day was only made possible by the presence of joint Anglo-French military forces.

Thankfully, there was little political unrest when

Dayspring arrived at Espiritu Santo, and the welcome from the islanders was tremendous. Aggie entered the small hospital for a minor operation and, as strong winds kept the boat harbour-bound, Ron worked in and around Santo. The New Testament in Bislama, a form of Pidgin English and one of the three official languages of the area, had been published in 1980 and the demand for literature was so great that some books had to be hidden away to save stock. Needless to say, all the villages on the island took their full quota of literature and tapes of personal testimony.

After Vanuatu, the *Dayspring* sailed to the Solomon Islands, reaching the capital, Honiara, in June. Almost immediately Ron faced problems. He expected to spend three months distributing his newly-acquired cargo of Bibles and Christian literature. Instead, he came up against local opposition. On earlier visits, Ron had been welcomed by a strong Bible Society committee, but now there was no visa, no committee, and the one Bible Society representative was half-hearted. The *Dayspring* crew had to wait for nearly three weeks to obtain a work permit from the government. When it finally arrived, it was for one month – starting from the day when the application had first been placed. That left Ron with exactly twelve days to distribute his load of Scriptures.

Aggie returned to New Zealand as June-Ann was sitting her university entrance exams and, facing up to the challenge before him, Ron wound his way through the vast network of lagoons and waterways. He managed to visit dozens of small villages, schools, and mission stations. 'Allan and Jeff would zoom off in the dinghy to sell Bibles and leave invitations for the evening meetings, which were held at strategic points in the lagoon. The majority of the people lived in man-made islands and it was an incredible task to get

149

the Scriptures to them, but we did it!'

After this unexpected adventure Jeff had to return home suddenly, leaving Ron and Allan to sail on alone into the trades. On the second night out, while Ron was on watch, the wind shifted making the alter tack more favourable. Rather than wake Allan, who was suffering from seasickness, Ron attempted to release the main sail boom by himself. It was a mistake – he hurt himself badly and lay helpless for a while before managing to crawl into the cockpit. Allan woke up and quickly made a makeshift bed in the galley, but it was obvious that Ron had broken his ribs. There was nothing else to do but return to the Solomons. Still the problems continued, as Ron explains: 'Allan did most of the steering and we arrived at Santa Ana in the early hours but, because of the trouble with customs, we had to hoist a yellow flag and anchor in the lagoon. The islanders kept away, and Allan had no help for ten days while he nursed me back to health.'

Ron was still unwell when he and Allan, accompanied by two helpers from Scripture Union, set off on a tour of the southern islands of Vanuatu. Ron was particularly keen to go there as, during the nineteenth century, the original *Dayspring* boats had enjoyed a remarkable fifty-year ministry in the area. Christians now praised God in a region that had once been populated by heathens and cannibals – although one remote island still practised a peculiar cult religion, with modern overtones.

The people of Tanna were awaiting the second coming of the god Jon Frum (thought to be a corruption of John from America), in an aircraft laden with luxury modern goods. The cult was obviously a left-over from the Second World War, when American troops were stationed in the area, but it had grown in popularity and the local pastors were anxious to 'fight back' with the Word of God. 'The original *Dayspring III*,' Ron explains, had never reached Tanna – it foundered on its way there in 1886, so the elders were really pleased when we finally arrived almost a century later! The local church loaned Allan a lorry and he was able to visit the whole island. His meetings attracted hundreds of people and they were particularly impressed by the "Jesus" film.'

By October Ron and Allan were back in Noumea, where they enjoyed a month of calm, sunny weather and some welcome assistance from local Christians. Ron was still suffering with his ribs but a dozen young lads from the Youth With A Mission ship *Anastasia* helped to do some of *Dayspring*'s paintwork. Mel Meehan and Bruce Perkins arrived later from New Zealand to act as crew for the journey home. Ron was pleased to arrive back in Auckland at the end of a very hard year, but he had the satisfaction of knowing that the *Dayspring* team had distributed more Scriptures than ever before.

The Russells took a well-earned rest in 1984, refitting the *Dayspring* as she nestled quietly on the Tamaki River. June-Ann was now sixteen and, like all teen-agers, she had a mind of her own. Aggie comments, 'For me, June-Ann has been an extraordinary type of girl. She wasn't really like other kids because she had a sheltered life, she lived in a cabin and did her correspondence course, so she didn't have to compete with other children. As she grew up it was sometimes hard to understand her. Once, when she was very down, I asked her what was wrong and she said, "Mum, I wish to goodness you and Dad would settle down and Dad would get a decent job!"'

Sadly, June-Ann did not share her parents' faith,

151

but she developed a strong moral code during this period, as Ron explains: 'June-Ann isn't religious but she doesn't like double standards. She tends to dislike youngsters who are very pious on the outside but do all sorts of things away from their parents. She used to come home from the youth clubs and get quite angry about that sort of thing.' However, although June-Ann was beginning to grow away from her parents' ministry, she was finding her own path in life, and it was during Ron and Aggie's 'rest year' that she passed her final exams with flying colours, and gained a university entrance to study social welfare.

The 'sabbatical' gave all three the chance to grow closer together, and towards the end of this much-needed break Ron wrote to friends, 'We have had a marvellous rest enjoying life together as a family, spoiling ourselves with the normal things on land that are not possible on a boat, like not having to worry constantly about weather changes and restless, rolling nights in an open bay.'

Ron also used the time to organise his sailing school. He wanted to keep it low-key and teach young people how to sail and have fellowship. He obviously had the right formula because, early in the new year, he held three 'Dayspring Summer Cruises' and they were highly successful.

Soon Ron and Aggie's thoughts were turning once again to their South Pacific mission. In a newsletter, Ron wrote, 'It is going to be difficult to get going again as life is most pleasant here in New Zealand. But the Word of God is needed in the islands and we know that with your prayers, love and support, we will find the strength and purpose to continue in that to which we are called.'

The call came from Fiji. The islanders were celebrating the 150th anniversary of the Gospel arriving on their shores, and they wanted the Russells to participate in the festivities. '*Dayspring* played a very vital part,' Aggie recalls, 'as the Methodist Church invited us to take pastors and Bible teachers out to the islands. It was great for us because, with the help of the church leaders and evangelists, we were able to really establish the Word of God in the remote areas. It was a partnership as we did the Scripture distribution while they talked to the villagers. We had a wonderful year, helping the Church to reach out to its own people.'

The Fijian tour gave the Russells a new sense of direction, and by early 1986 their ideas were changing. They began to realise that they could play a greater role in helping the churches to evangelise. Ron was keen to try this kind of work in the Solomon Islands. He and Aggie stayed in Suva for six weeks, waiting for a visa from the Solomons government, and nothing arrived. Eventually Aggie turned to Ron and said, 'Ron, I'm going to offer our services to the Methodists again, because it's no use sitting here.' Shortly afterwards a hurricane swept through the Solomons and both the South Seas Evangelical Church and World Vision asked Ron and Aggie to help with Scripture distribution. By this time, however, they had already committed themselves in Fiji.

It seemed that God wanted Ron and Aggie back in Fijian waters and they had a wonderful time taking pastors to the villages. They even returned to the Lau group, where Ron had been shipwrecked, and had a really fruitful ministry with the people of Ono-i-Lau. Many islanders remembered Ron's earlier visit to the region, and Aggie got on famously with the women. 'I lectured all through those islands, teaching the women how to come to Christ because, although they go to church every Sunday, many don't know Him as their own personal Saviour. And so I believe God wanted us in the Lau Islands.'

It was the first time that Ron had been back to the area since losing *Dayspring II* and he was still apprehensive. 'When we arrived, we anchored outside the passage. Teko, my friend from the island, was with us and he was quite confident that we would get through, although very few people have done it – it really is a nasty one. It was a worrying time, but we got inside the lagoon and we had a great stay with the people of Ono-i-Lau. I was a bit frightened coming out of the passage because there was another huge wreck – a 150-foot cargo boat – right in front of us. We almost had to touch it on our way out, and being so close to the place where *Dayspring II* went down made it a bit nerve-racking.'

That second tour of Fiji was particularly meaningful for the Russells. They had always maintained that the main thrust of their ministry was to 'sow the seed' so that God could 'reap the harvest', and at last, they began to see the fruits of their labour. At one village a man approached Ron and asked, 'Do you remember me?' Ron had to admit that he did not, and the man continued, 'You sold me this Bible.' As Ron looked inside the cover, he noticed some writing. It was the date on which the man had become a Christian, the same day he had purchased the Bible from Ron!

Aggie had similar experiences. As soon as she arrived at one of the outlying islands, a woman ran up and just bowled her over. She hugged Aggie and said, 'Oh, it's so good to see you.'

Puzzled, Aggie replied, 'But I don't know you.'

Then the woman told her, 'You don't know me, but I know you! I was in jail for two years on fraud charges, and a minister from my village brought me this Bible.' When she showed Aggie the Bible, she could see that it contained her signature and the date, 1973, Aggie recalled. 'At that time we had given Bibles to some of the pastors on the outlying islands – many of them didn't have Bibles for their pulpits. The pastor had obviously given his copy to this woman, who went on to say, "This is the Bible that brought me to Jesus Christ when I was in prison." It was wonderful to think that the Bible had helped her – she was on probation when we met, but she is now teaching crafts to the women in her village.' At another island, a young woman thanked Aggie for giving her a Bible when she was just ten years old. That same Bible had helped her through the first years of a difficult marriage.

From the Lau group Ron and Aggle sailed on to New Caledonia, finally returning to New Zealand where they met up with Ron's niece, Wendy Palmer. She was working her way around the world and the Russells, who had been invited to New South Wales by the local Bible Society, agreed to take her to Australia on the understanding that she would participate in the *Dayspring* activities. 'Wendy turned out to be an extremely enthusiastic sailor and a good crew,' Ron remembers. 'She was always last on deck and always doing odd jobs, and she was also keen to learn more about the Bible.'

The trip was a hectic one. 'The Bible Society had a pretty hot programme, and for a whole month Aggie and I worked very hard taking meetings throughout the area. June-Ann also joined us as she had finished college and was working with the social welfare. She had decided to take a couple of years off to do some travelling and was shortly to leave for Europe.'

Ron and Aggie were about to do some globe-trotting of their own. At the beginning of December, with

Dayspring safely moored in Sydney Harbour, they left the warm Australian sunshine to fly to the other side of the world. The Russells had accepted a Bible Society invitation to undertake a three-month tour of the United Kingdom. They were about to set foot on an island which was in the throes of one of its worst winters in years!

9.   Unexpected Developments

On Christmas Eve Ron and Aggie received a cable from Australia telling them that Wendy, who was still in Sydney, had made a decision for Christ. Ron comments, 'I shall always remember the day when Wendy first arrived at our house in Bucklands Beach. As soon as she sat down she told me that she couldn't understand why I had left London and gone to live such a different lifestyle. But she was keen to learn and she approached our ministry in a really intelligent way - she wasn't going to be persuaded overnight, she wanted to see if it was for real! However I think that, while she was on the boat, Wendy realised that we really did have a personal faith and, in the end, this was what she wanted, too.'

Wendy adds, 'I was greatly impressed by the way Ron and Aggie and their crew read the Bible every day, as I had never read it before. I soon became interested in learning more – Acts in particular gave me a good insight into how Paul came to lead people to Christ.' During her stay in Sydney, Wendy had been keen to enjoy all the delights this modern city had to offer. She made a number of friends at the local Bible Society headquarters – there were only a dozen or so people in the office but Wendy was really impressed by their enthusiasm – and she even began to think of starting a new life in Australia. Then, a few days before Christmas, Wendy tried to ring her family in London.

She was unable to get through and suddenly she felt very homesick.

Returning to *Dayspring*, she decided to read the Bible. 'I began to read Matthew and seemed to see pictures in my mind. I felt a lot of love and knew that, instead of fighting with my emotions, I should accept Jesus into my life and let Him take me wherever He wanted me to go.' Soon after this experience, Wendy went to a local church with a Christian friend, Morica, and during the service she publicly committed her life to Christ. Although she has now returned to London, where she works in accountancy, Wendy's visit to the Pacific marked a turning point in her spiritual life. Today her faith remains as strong as ever. 'I feel good knowing that I can look to God for assistance when things hurt me in the world – I feel happier knowing that He is in control of it. The love He gives to me just flows through, and it is such a wonderful gift.'

Ron and Aggie received Wendy's news at just the right time. They were in London enjoying an emotional reunion with Ron's mother and the rest of the family. 'The family treated us with great kindness, Ron recalls, 'and seemed to respect the stand we had taken over the years. My brothers and sisters had always had a general fear of God but the younger generation weren't so interested. It was a major breakthrough when my niece came to know the Lord.'

That winter was a busy one. From December to February Ron and Aggie travelled extensively in England, Wales, and Scotland, braving heavy snowfalls and treacherous conditions to visit schools and churches of all denominations. Aggie was impressed. 'I must say that the Bible Society was really "spot on" and we were very grateful for the way they worked our programme out.' The schedule was hectic, but the couple received a tremendous welcome wherever they went. One church group in Tunbridge Wells did their best to make them feel at home by organising a South Seas evening, complete with all the trimmings!

Many meetings attracted people who had first seen Ron and Aggie in 1977. At small Open Brethren Assemblies chapel in Gloucester an elderly lady told Aggie, 'I've travelled seventy miles especially to hear you and Ron. You may not remember me, but I met you ten years ago when you first came to England.' Others tackled similar distances. One young woman made her way from Southampton to a gathering in Birmingham, and a Fijian man drove 130 miles from the north of Scotland, where he was living with his Scottish wife, just to see the Russells.

It was heartening to discover that support for the *Dayspring* ministry was as strong as ever. When Ron and Aggie attended a gathering in Worthing they were introduced to two elderly sisters. One, a retired school-teacher, was eighty-two years old and she and her sister had collected their pennies as children to give to the Bible Society. They really were part of the 'old school', the mainstay of the Bible work overseas, and to this day, the sisters still send the Russells details about the Society's activities in their area.

The British press were particularly interested in the unusual visitors from warmer climes. Ron was able to explain some of the difficulties he and Aggie faced in the ministry and he told one Christian newspaper, 'Things are getting more political. Now we need permits, visas and other documents and many officials are reluctant to recognise our work as necessary.' He also commented on the changes he had noticed in the education system. 'I was no saint at school myself, but I do regret the trend in schools to do away with morning assemblies and memorising things like the Lord's Prayer. It was those memories that enabled me to become a Christian and have helped me over the years.'

Aggie was pleased to be able to share her honest thoughts about the need for support and she told reporters, 'I am always interested in the translation work because I believe that the Word of God must reach the island people in a language they can understand. I will always stress that – more translations must be done as there are some areas in the Pacific where they do not have the Bible in their own language.'

During their tour the couple visited the Swindon-based headquarters of the Bible Society and took the opportunity to explain the financial problems faced by the islanders. Ron comments, 'It's becoming even more difficult now – the people just don't have the money to pay for subsidised Scriptures so we have to find a way round the problem. One solution is to send slightly damaged Bibles that can be sold at a quarter of the usual cost.' Staff were quick to respond to this urgent Bible need. They had a stock of slightly imperfect Scriptures in the warehouse and promised to send the forty-eight precious cartons to the South Pacific. It was a tremendous belated Christmas present, as Ron explains: 'For years I've been trying to find a way of taking Scriptures to the islands at the right price – in line with the Bible Society's policy of providing Bibles that people can afford.'

The Society also made a pledge to raise £15,000 towards translation and distribution projects, including the production of Bibles with helps and Scripture selections for young people. In addition, staff organised a brief visit to Wyvern Television, a local TV studio, where Ron and Aggie recorded a twenty-minute interview with the Society's then Director for International Support, the Rev. Byron Evans (now minister of the Castle Street Welsh Baptist Church in London). The resulting VHS cassette video, 'Sailors for the Gospel', is still being used by the Society to generate interest in Ron and Aggie's ministry.

Once back in Australia the Russells set about refitting *Dayspring III*, perched high on the slips at the Cruising Yacht Club in Sydney. A young New Zealander, Harvey Olive, had been taking care of the boat while the couple were overseas. A skilled painter, he had been busy sanding and painting during his time on board. Harvey was a real answer to prayer, and within a matter of days, Ron and Aggie received even more help. Over a dozen energetic volunteers arrived to tackle the job of removing barnacles encrusted on the hull, leading the club's Vice-Commodore to remark that he had, 'never seen such an enthusiastic group of workers'.

'We had a great time in Australia,' Ron remembers, 'and the people were very generous. A lot of extra funds came through. One church gave us $3,500 and we were able to buy a radar and other navigational equipment, as well as a new mainsail. We were very impressed with the Bible Society in New South Wales the staff really were keen to get people to read the Bible.'

By early May 1987 the *Dayspring* was back in Fiji, and news of the coup led by Lieutenant-Colonel Sitiveni Rabuka had been announced. Ron and Aggie were about to embark on a voyage to Tuvalu as the Tuvaluan Bible, the first in that language, was finally ready and the Church wanted the couple to distribute copies in time for the Dedication Ceremony on 21 June. The translation, which had taken just fifteen years to complete, was a real breakthrough. Although 96 per cent of the 8,000 islanders were literate, they had always read the Bible in Samoan or English. Now at last they would be able to read God's Word in their own language. The political situation did not affect the trip, and Aggie recalls, 'Every time we left the port we had to tell the military where we were going but we never had any trouble.'

The voyage to Tuvalu was just like old times – there were forty-two cases of Bibles aboard the *Dayspring* and the crates were everywhere! Accompanied by an Australian crew and their old friend Mase, Ron and Aggie completed the journey in twelve days. Nevertheless time was running short, and they had to deliver the Scriptures to each of the islands in the group, scattered as they were over 500,000 square miles of the western Pacific. To complicate matters the crew were unable to use the dinghy because of the reefs, so the islanders had to paddle out to the yacht to collect the precious cargo.

There were some hair-raising moments as the Tuvaluans clung precariously to the side of the boat while the waves pounded around them. When the crates had been lowered into the small outrigger canoes, the islanders had to make their way back to the reef and wait for just the right wave to carry them safely into the quieter waters on the other side. 'The anchorages were wild,' Aggie remembers, 'and there we were in these little canoes going through the surfs with those cases – I used to close my eyes until we reached the beach!' Despite the problems the entire load – some 5,000 Bibles – was delivered on time. News of the Bibles' arrival was broadcast on Tuvalu Radio, and within hours the people were queuing up outside their pastors' homes to receive their own personal copy!

Because the Tuvaluan Bible had been produced by the Bible Society in New Zealand, its publication was jointly celebrated in Auckland and Funafuti. It was a time of great rejoicing for, with this latest translation, every one of the independent Pacific countries now had a complete Bible in its national language. The Tuvaluan celebrations were particularly impressive, although there had been similar rejoicing at the launch of the New Testament in 1977. Then, the pastor's wife had given birth to a son just half an hour before the dedication ceremony and the boy was immediately named Feagaiga Fou, which means New Testament. Ten years later the people once again gathered together to enjoy a week of feasting, dancing, and hymn-singing. Ron remembers the scene: 'We all gathered in the main church hall where the Bible was dedicated by 99 per cent of the people – the Prime Minister, the Government, and most of the islanders were there in their traditional Polynesian costumes. Each of the leaders stood up and made a speech and it was a privilege to be included in it all.'

This special event provided Ron and Aggie with an ideal opportunity to witness, and during their stay a number of islanders re-commited their lives to Christ. The people knew the Russells well and so they were able to hold numerous meetings. Many islanders seemed to hunger after the Word of God and were keen to study the Bible in small groups. Aggie comments, 'People are always asking for assurance – they want to know where they are going to go when they die. Ron and I are privileged to be able to share our faith with them and to encourage the villagers through our question time. If they haven't been taught the Word of God, this is where we come in. There is so much work to be done, not only distribution, but also getting through to the people so that they can have assurance of salvation, and know where they are going after they die.'

The new translation made a lot of difference for, each time Ron and Aggie were asked a question, they told the islanders to look it up in their new Bibles. The Russells could see the joy on the people's faces as they read the Old Testament stories in their own language for the very first time! Both Aggie and Ron were particularly grateful for Mase's help. Mase left his wife and family to accompany the *Dayspring* to Tuvalu and he was invaluable, for he spoke the language and was able to communicate with the islanders in just the right way. Aggie stresses, 'Mase is just like a son to us, so willing. He just does things quietly and we thank God over and over again for his testimony aboard the *Dayspring*.

The Russells were exhausted when they arrived back in Aggie's home town of Savusavu, but there was still much to do. The Tuvaluan Church had asked them to deliver three hundred Bibles to Kioa, a small Tuvaluan Island in Fiji. The load was to be taken by bus to a local jetty, where at one o'clock precisely, a boat would arrive to transport it across to the Tuvaluan population. Timing was all-important as the islanders were about to celebrate the opening of their new church and they wanted the new Bibles for the service. Ron and Aggie decided to ask George, a trusted Bible Society volunteer, to make the journey on their behalf.

George had first become involved with the Society through a prison distribution scheme. In 1976, when the Good News Bible was first published, Maika Bovoro had supplied some copies to all the prisons in Fiji. Three inmates, including George, were led to a new faith in Jesus Christ and two went on to study at Bible School in New Zealand. George was unable to leave Fiji because of his prison record, but he nevertheless became a dedicated voluntary worker, distributing

Scriptures throughout the interior.

Aggie was confident that George would meet the deadline but, thanks to her brother Peter, things did not go as smoothly as planned, George arrived at the bus station and the crates of Bibles were just about to be loaded when a soldier arrived on the scene. He was curious. 'What's in these boxes?' he asked.

Before George could reply Peter, who loved to have a joke, answered, 'Those are swords'. He was alluding to the familiar biblical phrase 'sword of the Spirit', but the soldier promptly called his colleagues. Before George could say a word, the militia opened the cases of Bibles and the 'ammunition' was rushed to the local police station!

George was frantic, and quickly alerted Aggie who rang through to explain the misunderstanding. Luckily, the Chief Inspector had been born in Kioa and spoke fluent Tuvaluan and soon realised what the 'weapons' really were. So impressed was he with the new translation that he took a copy for himself, leaving the over-zealous soldiers with 'egg on their faces'. In a scene reminiscent of the 'Keystone Cops' movies, they quickly loaded the boxes onto their Land-Rover and sped off to catch the bus. 'They only just caught up with it!' Aggie recalls. 'I was pretty angry with my brother, but it was quite funny really.'

After this adventure Ron and Aggie soon had other things on their mind. Despite the political upheaval in Fiji, the forty-eight cartons of Scriptures from England had finally arrived safe and sound. The Russells knew that the shipment would be gratefully received so they quickly set off on their travels once again, to an island some 200 miles from Suva. At one village only a few homes were occupied because most of the people had fled to the capital, so Ron and Aggie made their way to the Sunday school. The children welcomed their unexpected visitors and Aggie quickly asked, 'Hands up all those who don't have a Bible.' To her dismay, every child responded! She remembers, 'It was a joy to give them a Bible each. We also distributed hundreds of the "Good News for Modern Man" New Testaments at a price that the older children could afford. So in this way we found that the Bible Society had sent us a tremendous gift – I believe that God was at work in the minds of Byron Evans and all those at Bible House in England.'

For young people in the Pacific, the Bible is both a spiritual and an educational tool, as Ron points out: 'The children are brought up to read to a certain level in school but they have tremendous frustrations because, except for the tattered copies they use year in and year out, there are no books available. They are so pleased to get something new to read, and to be able to get the Word of God into their hands is extremely powerful because it's a virgin territory.'

The adults were also eager to take advantage of these subsidised Scriptures. At one of the coastal villages the local plantation manager would not allow the *Dayspring* team to go ashore with the Bibles but his assistant, a Fijian, told Ron and Aggie, 'Look, at two o'clock we will all be coming aboard.' Sure enough the workers arrived and, right up until nine o'clock at night, canoes and boats were going out to the yacht. Once on deck, the islanders just bought and bought and bought. Ron comments, 'During all my years in the Pacific, I have never doubted that God's Word is still needed in the area. Even though we have saturated many of the islands, the people still love to read the Bible.'

One Roman Catholic man who came aboard was looking for 'a very special book', a New Jerusalem Bible. His own copy had been stolen and he was delighted to find another among the Scriptures. He was even more delighted with the price – he had paid $49 for the original, but Ron had to charge him only $7 for the new, slightly-damaged version. A Methodist pastor also went away a happy customer. He purchased a concordance and his face gleamed as he told the Russells, 'It's the first time I've ever owned a concordance in my life.'

The popularity of the concordances convinced the Russells of the growing need for Bible study aids in the Pacific. 'When we first arrived in the islands, the church life was something for Sunday – the people were all Christians and didn't feel that they had to look at the Bible, that was the preacher's job. What a difference there is today! Many young people now get together to study the Bible – they are really hungry for concordances and Bible helps. There has been a tremendous breakthrough in the last ten years and we feel privileged to have been a small part of that.'

Aggie continues, 'The people really do need Bible study helps as well as Scriptures. We could have correspondence courses through the Bible Society as many islanders ask for this. There are so many openings for young people who want to read more about God's Word so as to strengthen their faith in Him.'

On their return to Savusavu, Ron and Aggie realised that news of the 'cheap Bibles' had spread, so they took advantage of this unique opportunity to witness and set up a stand in the market-place. They remained there for six weeks and Aggie's brother, Peter, could not believe the amount of counselling the couple were able to do just by selling Scriptures. One group of ladies bought something like 200 Bibles and New Testaments in English and Fijian. The material was obviously put to good use as, to this day, the ministry continues in Aggie's home town!

Aggie later wrote to Byron Evans in England: 'We do not begin to know how to thank you for the tremendous gift you've given us. At last we are able to give Bibles out freely, and also have enough to meet our needs. You should see the joy on the faces of these dear folk as they look at the different versions – they have never dreamt of owning a real leather Bible or a concordance. It's all too much, even for Ron and me.'

It was an uplifting time for Ron and Aggie, but Fiji's political problems continued and, following a second coup on 25 September the country was declared a Republic. Colonel Rabuka assumed full authority over national affairs and by October Queen Elizabeth II, who was attending the Commonwealth Conference in Vancouver, had accepted the resignation of Fiji's Governor-General. Ratu Sir Penaia Ganilau was the official symbol of her rule in the islands, and his departure signified the end of British sovereignty in that area. As an outsider Ron was particularly aware of the complexity of the situation: 'I always felt that Fiji was the most patriotic country of the whole Commonwealth. We've been into many villages, and, everywhere we went, we found the Queen's picture in every home. She was the paramount chief to the islanders, so the coup was quite a big break with tradition.'

Suddenly fear was everywhere – fear of violence, fear of oppression, and fear of unemployment and shortages. There was ample reason for the general mood of despondency for, since the first coup, foreign exchange reserves and the value of property had fallen and investments had dried up. One of Fiji's greatest assets, its tourists, had disappeared and in a few short months hotels had become deserted, many small business had been forced to close, and a large number of people were out of work. The all-important sugar crop was also at risk because of sabotage and boycotts. Fiji had been the focus of trade routes in the Pacific, but, for the first time in recent history, there was a very real threat of long-term destabilisation in the whole area. Such was the concern of the churches that the Anglican Bishop of Polynesia, the Right Rev. Jabez Bryce, spoke publicly of the 'demon of fear' set loose in the land. He declared that only the love of God could cast out such terrors and called for 4 October to be set aside as a national Day of Prayer.

'At that time,' Aggie remembers, 'the people, both Fijian and Indian, were hungry for God's Word and looked for stability amid the chaos. It was a privilege for us to share Christ with them. It really brought the Indians out and there were lots of enquiries – they wanted to find out more about this Living God.' Ron did not have permanent Fijian citizenship so it was agreed that he should stay on *Dayspring* while Aggie ran the Bible stall with the help of George, the Fijian volunteer. One day a local Indian tailor came aboard. He said he had been to a Methodist school but had not taken much notice of religion. Ron suggested that he read the Bible again, to see what God was trying to say. He was very keen to do so, and bought a couple of Bibles for himself and his children.

There was an added incentive to read the Bible at this time, as only a month earlier, the Bible Society had launched a common language version of the New Testament in Fijian. Until this time the people had read the Scriptures in English because the Fijian Bible – some 150 years old – was almost impossible to understand. This modern translation was particularly well received, and the Society was also involved in the distribution of New Testaments and Scripture portions in Hindi.

The Russells finally returned to New Zealand in November, June-Ann was still in Europe and Ron and Aggie were unsure of their own future in the South Pacific. They wondered if *Dayspring* should venture further afield, perhaps to the West Indies. By the end of the year, however, things were beginning to look brighter and an element of calm had been restored in Fiji. Ron comments, 'God's Word is really honoured in the Fijian islands, and the people are trying to get back to the basics of the Bible. Many Westerners are living in a grey area, but we can't live by our own rules. For my own part, I still believe that the Word of God is the only basis for growth and stability. We've seen this in places like Tuvalu, in Fiji with the coup, in fact anywhere where the people are trying to get back to the principles of the Bible.'

10.   New Opportunities

Steve Burmester, a young graduate, left England on 19 February 1988 to travel to the other side of the world. Stopping first at Hawaii and Fiji, he was on his way to join Ron and Aggie in New Zealand. Steve had first met the Russells during their tour of the United Kingdom, as his future father-in-law, Ken Needham, preached at the Capernwray Bible School in England and he and his wife Eva knew the couple very well. At that time Steve was studying for a Physiology Degree at Leeds University, but he was keen to do some Christian work overseas so he kept in touch with Ron and Aggie. When he finally completed his studies it was decided that he would join the *Dayspring* for a few months.

He was very excited about this forthcoming venture, but on arrival in Auckland Steve realised that life aboard *Dayspring* was not quite what he had expected. He remembers his first few weeks vividly. 'The first thing that struck me was the vast amount of work Ron put into keeping *Dayspring* in shape. He would spend every day down on the yacht doing a wide variety of tasks – it was a never-ending job. I spent six weeks working with him, and finally we brought the boat out onto the slipway for ten days where we scraped down the hull and painted it with anti-foul. It was a real training time for me – it meant that I had to get my hands dirty and do some dedicated hard work. It

taught me a lot of self-discipline and self-sacrifice, all
of which was essential to the later work in the islands.'

Despite the physical grind, things were going well
for the ministry. The funds kept coming and the
various donations allowed Ron and Aggie to add an
electric auto pilot and a new VHF radio telephone to
Dayspring. By early spring they had no doubt as to
their destination, for they had finally received a clear
invitation to share the Gospel with the people of
Vanuatu. The plan was to visit the outlying islands in
the group during May to September, going on to New
Caledonia in the autumn.

Allan Pfeiffer, the only experienced sailor free to
travel at the time, had agreed to accompany Ron on
the first leg of the journey to Fiji. There were also two
other crew members. The first was Les Price, a retired
metalworker from Nelson in the south island of New
Zealand, who had just finished building his own 28-
foot steel yacht and wanted some sailing experience
before he embarked on a ministry of his own. The
second was John Deboer, an engineer with the New
Zealand Electricity Board, who turned out to be an
excellent seaman.

Dayspring sailed out of Auckland Harbour on 19
April, arriving in Fiji some nine days later. It was six
o'clock on Sunday morning and Suva was blissfully
quiet as Ron laid anchor. It had been a rough journey
and the men were grateful to be able to take a rest and
enjoy some Bible study and worship together. The
next day, after a visit to Customs, they sailed on to
Ron's usual mooring at the Tradewinds Hotel, but
just as they were lowering the anchor, the prop shaft
became entangled in some mooring line, Allan quickly
donned a wet suit and went down to investigate. He
had to cut the line free, and as he was coming up the
lady proprietor of the hotel called out, 'You might as

172

well cut the rest while you're down there, I won't be needing them'. Allan was happy to oblige, and the crew thought no more about the incident. They stayed in Suva for a week, stocking up with Scriptures before setting out to Lautoka on the west coast, the most strategic springboard for their trip to Vanuatu.

Everything went smoothly and on the Thursday morning, just before Ron was due to visit Customs, the men enjoyed a brief time of Bible study. The passage was from James 4.13–17: 'Now listen to me, you that say, "Today or tomorrow we will travel to a certain city, where we will stay a year and go into business and make a lot of money." You don't even know what your life tomorrow will be! You are like a puff of smoke, which appears for a moment and then disappears. What you should say is this: "If the Lord is willing, we will live and do this or that." But now you are proud, and you boast; all such boasting is wrong. So then, the person who does not do the good he knows he should is guilty of sin.' The passage stimulated some lively debate, but no one realised how prophetic it would actually turn out to be!

As soon as the Bible study was over, Ron said, 'Right, I'm off to Customs. We should be clear to get away by one o'clock.' Expecting to leave within a matter of hours, the crew busied themselves with odd jobs around the boat until Ron returned. When he turned up two hours later, however, he looked very worried. The men asked what was wrong and he told them, 'You're not going to believe this, but I've just been arrested!'

Ron related the sad story. On arrival at the Customs office he had been told that his name was on a summons. He was to appear in court the very next day. The reason for this sudden entanglement with the authorities was the incident with the mooring lines in

Suva. The lines cut by Allan had not belonged to the Tradewinds Hotel at all, but were the property of a local resident and he wanted to take the matter further. As skipper of the *Dayspring*, Ron had to appear as a witness. The delay was particularly ironic because of the Bible passage, but the crew found it hard to understand why God was allowing them to be held up in this way. They had already been delayed in Suva because the Bibles had not been delivered on time, and now this!

By the next day, however, everything became crystal clear. The police van arrived early in the morning and Ron, accompanied by Les, went off to sort things out. The others stayed aboard *Dayspring* waiting eagerly for news, but when Ron phoned them later that evening, they were in for a surprise. Ron had been met at the court-house by a Bible Society representative who had told him, 'Thank goodness you haven't gone, Ron. There's been trouble in Vanuatu and the Bible Society supporters there phoned me yesterday to say: "Please don't let Ron and Aggie come because we're not ready for them yet, there's been the worst political riot here in the capital city, the worst we've ever seen!"' If the crew had kept to their original timetable, they would have sailed straight into the middle of all the chaos.

Steve remembers: 'All things work together for the good of those who love God. We were kept safe in Suva, and Aggie came across and sorted everything out, as only she can. The incident with the mooring lines was cleared up within a few days and we were finally able to set sail four days later. That's the kind of adventure that Ron and Aggie come across in their ministry – they're so dependent on God for everything. I don't want to make them into superheroes but they have an amazing devotion to the Lord Jesus in their work and He takes care of them in one way or another!'

Although news of the trouble in Vanuatu came as a surprise, the people had suffered greatly in recent years. Two of their main exports had been badly hit. The coconut oil mill on the largest island, Espiritu Santo, had been burned during the 1980 uprising, bringing exports of that particular commodity to a halt. In addition, copra production had gone into decline because many of the coconut plantations were ageing. To add to the nation's economic problems, there had been three catastrophic cyclones in less than eighteen months. The most recent, in February 1987, had caused widespread devastation, making thousands homeless and ruining crops. Nevertheless, the uprising in Port Vila blew over quickly, so the *Dayspring* team were able to continue with their original plans to visit Vanuatu.

At last Ron was on his way, but the most important cargo was still not aboard. The Bislama New Testament and Psalms had only recently been published and the 3,000 copies allocated to the *Dayspring* ministry were to be shipped to Santo. Ron headed straight for the island, but once there, he faced problems yet again. 'The shipment had been delayed, but we were able to get 250 copies that had been air freighted, so we set out on a tour of the Banks and Torres Islands. We had great co-operation from the Santo Bible Society translation/action group, who had arranged for three local volunteers – Philip Bane, Toswell Vira, and Jimmy Alrich – to help us. They all turned out to be tireless workers and we had a most successful trip, in spite of the bad weather and difficult anchorages.'

One morning stood out in Ron's memory, 'We were

up bright and early to get to Lo in the Torres Islands, and when we arrived at six-thirty a.m. the bells were ringing to announce our arrival. But we couldn't land – the surf, crashing onto the reef, forced us to sail away to the east to the Banks and it really was a very sad moment for us.'

Navigating in and out of the reefs was a particular problem, despite the fact that one member of crew always went to the top of the mast to guide Ron through the passages. Steve realised just how deceptive the reefs could be when, on one occasion, he took on the role of lookout. From his elevated position, he had a perfect view of both the water's depth and a passage leading to an inviting little lagoon. The boat was surrounded by coral heads so Ron started motoring in very slowly until, all of a sudden, Steve yelled a warning. He had just seen a green coral head lurking right up in front of *Dayspring*. Ron didn't hear what he was saying until it was too late, and as he started to go astern, the boat thrust sideways, edging on to the coral head and grinding to a halt. At first everyone was bewildered and Aggie began to let off steam, but it was high tide and still light, so the men were able to dive down and have a look at the damage. Luckily, everything was fine - they were only resting on the reef and the high tide cleared them by midnight, but it was a harrowing experience just the same.

Steve was fascinated by the sea life in this tropical paradise, and he recalls, 'I used to love the fact that the dolphins would come in and play on the bow of the boat no matter what the weather.' The playful creatures also led him to a deeper spiritual awareness, as he explains: 'Sometimes, when we had been hit by a bad storm and had to try and point up into the wind because of *Dayspring*'s small keel, the going was very difficult. Once, the engine was full on to stop us going

176

back onto the reef, the bow was tipping into the waves and everything seemed to be going wrong. The hatches hadn't been tied down and the covers had blown away, and Ron asked me to go out and tie the sail. I edged my way forward, the waves tossing over me, but then I glanced over into the sea and saw dolphins playing ahead of the boat. It was poignant to me because they were enjoying themselves while we were battling to get away from the danger of the reef. Then I realised that, even in the middle of the storm, Jesus can take your eyes away from the battle to look at His joy and peace.'

During that tempestuous voyage, Aggie obviously remained true to the vow she had made in the Austral Islands years before – never to lose faith in the Lord no matter what the conditions. Steve remembers that, even in the roughest storm, she always stayed calm and collected!

Although the weather was often bad, the *Dayspring* team visited most of the islands in the Vanuatuan group, and were able to report record sales. They eventually distributed a grand total of 1,000 English Bibles, 1,500 English New Testaments, 3,000 Bislama New Testaments and Psalms, and 5,000 portions of Scriptures, as well as numerous Scripture Union booklets and tapes. The Melanesian islanders are very shy people, but they were always pleased to see *Dayspring* and were gentle and amenable. However, they were relatively poor and could not provide the lavish hospitality of their Fijian brothers. A typical menu in the villages consists of 'laplap', a sweet pudding containing bits of vegetable, plus the traditional Kava.

Ron and Aggie were used to this simple life-style, but Steve experienced something of a culture shock, as he explains: 'We usually ended up staying the night with the villagers, sleeping on a mat on the floor accompanied by a couple of chickens. It was quite an experience for me because, as an Englishman, I am used to my home comforts! It's a completely different way of life, material goods don't really figure at all. Most of the villages have a small chapel of sorts, and there is usually someone in charge of the people's spiritual needs – a sort of pastor, but not a full-time minister as such. And yet there are some amazing Christians there, they really are dedicated and were thrilled to receive the New Testament in their very own language. It made all the travelling worthwhile.'

Steve left the *Dayspring* in June. He had arranged to work in India for a while before returning to England for a very special occasion, his wedding! He married his wife, Joanna, at Capernwray Hall in September and was very moved to receive a telegram from Ron and Aggie. Written in Bislama, it quoted Deuteronomy 24.5: 'When a man is newly married, he is not to be drafted into military service or any other public duty; he is to be excused from duty for one year, so that he can stay at home and make his wife happy.' Steve is now living with Joanna in Cheshire. He works in finance and during his spare time he shares his experiences of the *Dayspring* ministry with numerous church groups.

By July, Les had also left *Dayspring* and Ron and Aggie were joined by two new crew members, Eric Lindbeck from America and Mark Welch from Germany. The small team completed the tour of Vanuatu and set off for New Caledonia, arriving at Noumea in October. There had been trouble in the area earlier in the year and clashes between islanders and the local gendarmes had become a major topic during the run-up to the French presidential elections.

178

Ron and Aggie encountered no problems and were able to spend a delightful month enjoying a reunion with old friends like Peter Compton. Christian fellowship was very much in evidence in Noumea. Some two years before an exhibition of Bibles and Scriptures had been held there to mark the tenth anniversary of the Bible Society auxiliary. All the churches, Roman Catholic and Evangelical, had been involved in giving assistance to the Bible Society committee.

Ron and Aggie arrived in New Zealand in November, having completed yet another 'tour of duty' in the Pacific. It had been an eventful year for the couple and for Bible Society in Suva, where staff had welcomed a new Executive Director, Solomone Duru, and various other recruits. During the annual Fijian Bible Week celebrations in August the Society took part in the very first Christian Book Fair to be held in Suva.

Other organisatons were also involved and a representative reported, 'It was a beautiful picture of oneness in the common goal of sharing God's Word with all.' By the end of 1988, the Society was engaged in a number of new ventures, including a Christian Youth Concert in Suva and the production of easy-to-read Gospel stories for primary schools in the Pacific.

Back in Auckland, Ron and Aggie still had much to do, and just after Christmas 1988 Ron and John Deboer left for Nelson to begin major work on *Dayspring*'s hull. At the time of writing, the Russells were planning to spend 1989 doing major refits to the boat and, in 1990, to return to French Polynesia for an extended visit, calling at the Cook Islands, Samoa, and Fiji on the way back. They expect to be away for some two years. Ron comments: 'Several times we've thought about the end, but God keeps taking us back and the goodwill is still there, for the common people all know *Dayspring* – she's pretty much a household

179

name now. Aggie and I are both reasonably healthy, although we're obviously older and we do get tired more quickly, but I feel just as fit as I did ten years ago, and the Lord continues to fund us! We have a quiet assurance that we will continue to get on with the job. *Dayspring III* has proved to be the boat for the task and we will continue to use her until we see a clear sign to the contrary.'

Despite her aversion to the sea, Aggie is also eager to continue. 'I get seasick, I get fed up with the reefs. I never know if I am going back to a particular island, so I tell the people they must listen now. But as long as the Lord gives us health, we want to go on. I have arthritis and those companion steps are pretty hard to climb. Because we have no portholes on the boat, I have to go on deck to throw away the garbage. The money and the crew will always come, I have never doubted that for a moment, but health is more important, and that's the Lord's department.'

And what of the many people who have played a vital part in Ron and Aggie's story? Their daughter, June-Ann, at twenty-one has returned from her travels and is living in a flat in Auckland, working at the Social Welfare office and hoping to return to England in the not too distant future. 'We were really surprised when June-Ann wanted to break out on her own,' Aggie comments, 'but I think it was the best for her – we trusted the Lord to look after her. When she was travelling in Europe she wrote and told us of all the friends she had met. She really learned a lot and it was a great experience for her to meet so many different people.'

Maika Bovoro has also travelled far. No longer with World Vision, he is now working amongst the aborigines in Australia as Dean of an Aboriginal Bible

School, and one of his sons is also with him. The Russells will always have a high regard for Maika, for Aggie recollects, 'In the early years, when we were young missionaries working in very difficult islands, Maika gave us great encouragement. He was so liked and respected and, as the Bible Society's General Secretary, he used to love working in the field. He would come with us to the islands and teach and go on tirelessly through the night, sharing the Bible with the people and ministering to them. He wasn't at home in the office, he felt that God wanted him out in the islands. Now he is working with the people he loves.'

The various volunteers who have helped to crew the *Dayspring* are also a vital part of the ministry. Ron remembers, 'As well as Mase, we've had a number of folks over the years including Allan Pfeiffer, who came along at the right time and stuck to it. He learned how to sail and how to take the rough with the smooth – the drudgery of the long hours at the wheel and the seasickness, as well as the adventure. Also Mike Hunsberger, who came from the beginning and really dedicated himself to the work – he has now gone back to Canada and is married with a family, he's also running a sailing school in British Columbia. Rod Klassan sailed with us from 1986–87 and he was a great help, he's now helping Mike with his school. Then there was Peter Thomas, who was really enthusiastic, a good Bible teacher and a great administrator; he's heading a Bible School at the new Capernwray Centre in New Zealand. Dave Harding, who stuck it out with Mike for six months in the Cook Islands, got married in 1987. There was also John Deboer, who was with us in Vanuatu last year and is still helping us refit the boat in Nelson; he is very faithful and dedicated to the Lord's work. These are the crew we thank God for, and the many others who have come and gone during our years of service aboard the *Daysprings*.'

Ron and Aggie are always eager to welcome volunteers to the ministry, but they often find that it attracts a 'mixed bag' of folk. 'What we're looking for in a crew are those who are able to go on deck and, when the anchor's down, pick up boxes of Bibles and go ashore. Sometimes they have to sit through long hours by a Bible table, perhaps not talking to a soul while the meetings are going on. Over the years there haven't been more than about six or seven who have been absolute all-rounders like Allan, but there have been a few who have stuck by us and we're very grateful for those.'

Because of disappointments in the past, Ron has learned to be hard when interviewing possible helpers. He has been known to grill them for hours, telling them how hard the conditions are 'in the field', and pointing out the need for complete dedication. Needless to say, some are still enthusiastic to accompany him, so he has to take them on trust and hope that they will turn out to be permanent crew. Ron remembers one particular volunteer who had been writing to him for two years. He was in the coastguard and came from missionary parents in Africa. His credentials were absolutely ideal, or so they seemed.

Ron takes up the story: 'This young man arrived and when we rowed across to the boat I told him to tie the dinghy up. You should have seen the knot he tied! I asked him what he was doing on the coastguard if he didn't know how to tie a knot and only then did he inform me that he'd never been on a boat – as a coastguard he had been on a radar station up in the Hebrides in the north of Scotland somewhere. So I said, "Well, I'm going to give you a crash course on knots." After dinner he was very excited and asked me

182

where we were going. I told him that, in a few days, we'd be getting the Bibles on board and going to the island of Kandavu. "Oh," he said, "where's that?" That really amazed me, because he'd been writing to me for years and yet he didn't know where the fourth largest island in the Fiji group was.'

Although he was becoming suspicious of his new recruit, Ron decided to give him a chance and the team set off for their destination. Once at Kandavu, however, things got worse! As was usual in Fiji, the meeting finished well after midnight, and throughout the evening Ron could see the young man's face getting longer and longer. He did not get involved with the village lads, but sat in a corner and only did what Ron told him to do.

After some five days, Ron took the young man to one side and, after a short prayer, said, 'Come on now, what's the problem?'

To Ron's amazement, the young man burst into tears. He told Ron, 'I just don't understand your ministry, it's crazy! We go out at four o'clock but don't start till nine p.m., we don't get any sleep because we arrive in the early hours of the morning. It wasn't like that in Africa – we had the meeting arranged for seven o'clock, had our supper, went to the destination where everyone would be waiting, and Dad would get up and give his talk. By eight-thirty p.m. we were home again!'

Ron tried to explain that the whole idea of the work in the islands was to be available to the people and to adapt to their culture, but the young man replied, 'Oh, I can't stand it!' He caught the plane a few days later and that was the last Ron saw of him.

'Volunteers often come to me,' Ron comments, 'expecting me to have a magic wand waved when they arrive in the islands, even though they can't share their faith in New Zealand or wherever. They think that it will be a piece of cake when they get out among the villagers, and this is absolute nonsense. It's very important for young people to know that it's a waste of time moving out to the mission field unless they have conquered their fear of evangelising on their own doorstep.'

The *Dayspring* ministry is certainly a demanding one, and when they return home to Auckland the Russells treasure the opportunity to have a few months to unwind. 'In the early days,' Ron explains, 'we would sit down with the prayer list and go ringing around within the first week or so, but we don't do that any more. When we do meet up with old friends we find that, before long, we're taking lots of meetings and we get too tired when we return to the islands, so we just let things develop slowly now. The Open Brethren Assemblies that have supported us over the years are very kind when we get home – they don't demand us to give a report straight away.'

'Some even invite us to go on holiday,' Aggie continues, 'but my holiday is in my four walls, because I love to be able to come home and shut the door. There aren't any doors on the boat – I really enjoy the privacy of our bedroom, that's a holiday to me! We treasure our cottage very much, and it doesn't move! During the first few days at home, if I hear a tap dripping or see a light on, I think, "Oh no, it's a waste." But of course it isn't such a waste in a house. It's a real luxury not to have to worry about these things.'

A possible drawback, depending on one's point of view, is the lack of contact with the neighbours. Aggie comments, 'I'm not home long enough to get to know them very well. Often, after we've been away for months at sea, they have moved, and then I am busy and catching up with all the correspondence and cleaning the house. However, I do get a chance to meet up with some of the locals when I take the bus into Howick town to do some shopping. I've got to know quite a few of the senior citizens over the years and when they see me they say, "Gosh, where have you come from this time?" The majority don't even know Christ, but I have the tremendous opportunity to tell them where I've been and what I've been doing and when I'm going out again, and they think I'm a millionaire! They don't realise that God is the millionaire – we don't like to tell people our needs, but He has provided in remarkable ways over the years.'

Ron too finds that his unique lifestyle acts as an ideal introduction. 'Over the years I've found that we are privileged to have lived such an adventurous life. It's not difficult to start up a conversation with people who are curious to know what we're doing, running about the Pacific. Nevertheless, I think I've learned not to get into talking for too long, but rather to hint at things gradually, otherwise people are overawed by it all. It's very effective if we just tell them a little at a time, and they get very curious. We're fortunate to be able to share our faith with people from all walks of life.'

In time, the couple may develop some kind of local ministry. The sailing school is doing well and, according to the Bible Society in New Zealand, there is still a growing need for evangelism in the country. A national opinion poll, undertaken for the Society in 1986 by a Church of Christ minister, stated that some 85 per cent of New Zealanders own a Bible but only 11 per cent read it regularly. The poll, based on a randomly selected sample of 1,500 people aged 18 years and over, prompted the Society's General

Secretary, Colin Reed, to say: 'After working in New Zealand since 1846, the Bible Society's task is far from finished. We have a great deal of work to do to supply the Bible to the growing group who do not have one, and an even greater task in convincing New Zealanders that God's Word is the answer to all their needs.

Ron and Aggie may well decide to remain in Auckland, staying on call from year to year to undertake any necessary work in the Pacific islands. The needs are still great. The Bible Society in Suva faces a huge translation problem as the complete Bible is only available in 16 of the 207 local languages. A general lack of funds delays progress but dedicated Christians are battling against the odds. Aggie fondly quotes the case of one man in Vanuatu who spends his time in a mud-floor hut, where he is trying to translate the Bible into his tribal language. She and Ron look forward to the day when every Pacific islander will have the Scriptures in his or her own vernacular tongue.

Whatever happens the Russells will continue to reach the unreached, wherever they may be. Aggie has the last word: 'I believe that the Bible must be read and studied by the individual, because we can get so much preaching and read so many books about people's lives and testimonies, and we can dote upon heroes who have come to know Christ in miraculous ways. But the Bible is very relevant for each individual to find out for themselves what God is saying to them personally. As the Bible states: "Yes, grass withers and flowers fade, but the Word of our God endures for ever," (Isaiah 40.8).'

Appendix: Bible Society – Sharing God's Word

Over 64,000 people join the Christian Church every day but, particularly in developing countries, many cannot afford a Bible. There are other difficulties – although the number of languages and dialects into which at least one complete book of the Bible has been translated has reached 1,907, there is still a long way to go. Estimates of the total number of languages in the world are just over 6,000. Consequently, more than 4,000 languages still need to be tackled if all peoples are to have access to the message of the Scriptures.

This is the challenge facing the United Bible Societies (UBS) today. Founded over forty years ago, the UBS is an association of national Bible Societies – more than 100 around the globe. Central to each Bible Society's purpose is the task of making the Bible available to people in a language they can understand and at a price they can afford.

Translation – the starting point

With a possible 4,000 languages still to go, Bible Societies seem to face a daunting task. Yet in fact they have an impressive track record in achieving results. They are currently engaged in 567 new translation projects. Of these, 282 are in the Asia-Pacific region, 61 are in the Americas and Europe, and 224 are in Africa. In over 300 of the languages, some part of the

Bible is being translated for the very first time; in other cases, the translations are either modern versions or revisions of existing texts.

Such progress is made possible through a dedicated team of translators and specialist staff, who work day in and day out to provide Scriptures in a variety of mother-tongues. Modern technology, particularly word processors and other computer applications, ensure efficiency and economy in production. The UBS General Secretary, Dr Cirilo Rigos, comments: 'While the task of translating the Scriptures is an enormous one, it is exciting to see that each year Scripture translation agencies get closer to their goal of making the Word of God available to all people.'

A co-operative effort

Today's global network has its origins in a meeting of the Religious Tract Society in London in 1802. At that meeting a visitor was telling the committee of the desperate need for Welsh Scriptures in the thriving Welsh language churches and schools. During the discussions which followed, the secretary, Joseph Hughes, spoke the now famous words: '... if for Wales, why not also for the Kingdom and the World?' Two years later, on 7 March 1804, the British and Foreign Bible Society held its first meeting. Within a few short years, the Society was supplying Scriptures to Africa and had established agencies in Europe and Asia.

Throughout the nineteenth century, sister Societies sprang up and worked closely with the British and Foreign Bible Society. These included the American Bible Society, founded in 1816, which provided Scriptures for outreach in Latin America and the Middle East. By the early part of the twentieth century, many of the sister Societies had also established agencies, and there was an urgent need for international co-operation. This led to the creation of the UBS in 1946. The UBS general office, now located in Reading, England, co-ordinates the activities of Bible Societies around the world.

Getting the Scriptures out

Because parts of the world are still very remote, Bible distribution is often both difficult and expensive. Some Scriptures are transported by air but most are taken by road and rail to their destination – the various national Bible Societies rely heavily on their networks of volunteers who travel to isolated regions to take Scriptures to those in need. Despite the problems, however, Scriptures are delivered at a staggering rate – during 1986–87 alone some 13.5 million Bibles, 11.4 million New Testaments, and millions of Scripture portions and selections were distributed worldwide. Yet demand continues to outstrip supply.

In addition to the obvious tasks of translation, production and distribution, UBS member Societies are also involved in promoting the effective use of Scriptures. They provide books, study programmes and materials for evangelists, as well as Bible stories for children and New Reader material for people learning to read. They are involved in a wide range of activities, from emergency projects in national disaster areas to the provision of Scripture selections for the rehabilitation of prisoners. In a way, Bible Societies are publishing houses, but publishers with a very special mission: to enable the Word of God to reach the hands of people everywhere.

The future

It is estimated that during the next twenty-five years the world population, particularly in the developing countries, will increase by over one billion. Bible needs will be great and there will be proportionately fewer affluent people to support the underprivileged. Nevertheless, the national Bible Societies owe much to the ordinary Christians of the world, who give freely of their time, energies, money and prayer. They give generously today and they will help to meet the challenges of tomorrow.